Visits of Gertrude Bell to Tur Abdin

by Dale A. Johnson

New Sinai Press

Dedicated to

**The Aydin family of Gunduk Shukro who carry on the
tradition and prayers of Syriac Christians**

With special thanks

To

Malphono Isa Gulten

Library of congress Cataloging-in-
Publication Data
New Sinai Press
Visits of Gertrude Bell to Tur Abdin
C Travel, Orthodox,, Christianity, Turkey

ISBN 978-0-6151-5567-8

Manufactured in the United States of
America

First edition
September 2007

barhanna2001@yahoo.com

Table of Contents

Note:

Summaries are from Bell's book *Amurath to Amurath* in 12 point Garamond font

Diary entries lead with mm/dd/yyyy in 12 point Georgia font

Letters are indicated by name of day, month, and day 16 point bold Georgia font

All material and photos are courtesy of University of Newcastle Library

Introduction

I was about the same age as Gertrude Bell when I first went to Tur Abdin. I spent my 41st birthday on the Mountain of the Servants (Tur Abdin), the same age as Gertrude. That was in 1990, 81 years after Gertrude Bell first visited Mor Gabriel monastery. Today we approach the centennial celebration of Gertrude's famous visit. She was the first one to systematically record by photograph and written account the vast treasures of Oriental Christianity in Tur Abdin hidden behind the veil of Islam. As an orientalist she was superbly qualified to study, comment, and present this land of forgotten Christians. She brought along with her Sir William M. Ramsey who probably needed her wisdom and guidance to navigate the Ottoman labyrinth of customs and language. Sir Ramsey was a scholar of the first rank, but Bell's intimate knowledge and passion for the region far outshone the genius of Ramsey who went on to become a world authority on the Christian world of antiquity. His "Beatrice" was Gertrude and together they wrote a masterpiece on Christian archeology, architecture, linguistics, and culture titled "A Thousand and One Churches." The Turkish Ottoman empire of the northern regions of the Euphrates and Tigris rivers was in some ways more the Holy Land than Palestine to the south. This was the region of Paul of Tarsus, the Churches of Ephusus, Phyrgia, and Laodocia. Gertrude guided Sir Ramsey. It is the land of the New Testament Church which fled north after the fall of Jerusalem into the lands that we know today as northern Syria and Turkey. This is where Christianity experimented, flourished, and was persecuted along the east west axis trade routes from

Constantinople to China. By the 4th century, Christianity had become the official religion of Asia Minor. Most Christians spoke Aramaic., the language of Jesus. The more educated one spoke, read, and wrote Greek, Aramaic, and even Latin. Much of the Church retained its Semitic character. After the rise of Islam though, this Semitic form of Christianity was swept under the carpet of Islam. It did not die but their lack of access to the west eventually caused serious divisions in theology and mutual understanding. The early Church council were attended only by a minority of Bishops and church leadership. Marutha of Maiferqat reported that of over 2000 Bishops, most of whom lived under Persian rule East of the Euphrates, only a few more than 300 Bishops attended the council. Later councils were essentially the same demographically. Yet, the Bishops who did not show up eventually list power and often were considered heretics, which resolved the issues of lack of majority in the decision-making process. Western Bishops ascended to power by default if you look at the issue from a demographic point of view.

It was this hidden and much maligned eastern and Semitic form of Christianity that Gertude Bell rediscovered in 1909. For this we are grateful. Of course the world knew of the existence of these interesting and enthnocentric Christians. Moses of Mardin showed up in Rome in the early 1500s. Most clergy in the Vatican did not know there were Christians in the regions to the East. Moses has to show his manuscripts in Syriac/Aramaic to demonstrate that Christianity had been alive but ill in the Moselm East. In the 17th century Jesuits show up in China thinking they are the first Christians to arrive in the Sino capital of Sian only to discover that

Aramaic speaking Christians had been there for a 1000 years making significant contributions to Chinese culture.

So it was not as if Christianity of the eastern form had been completely forgotten. It had been periodically remembered and then the West would drift off to theological sleep again. But Gertrude Bell's work may assist in helping the West to NEVER forget. Her pictures are vivid and a permanent record of the existence of a form of Christianity that has never died and in fact has preserved a primitive form of spiritual DNA, if you will, that goes back to the time of the historical Jesus. No other form of Christianity can lay claim to that kind of direct linguistic and cultural link. Everyone else in an adopted child of the Semitic parentage of Christianity. Christianity, after all is not a religion of the West. It is a religion of the East. Latin Christianity can only indirectly inherit the spiritual genes of Jesus. Greek Christianity can only contract by theological translation the words of the Master, and it can only do that imperfectly. That is not to say that Aramaic forms of Christianity are perfect. Far from it. But what is preserved in the Christianity of Upper Mesopotamia, in the region of Tur Abdin, is a fossil that has come back to life by the aid of people like Gertrude Bell. She understood the importance of telling the world about these forgotten Christians. Because of her a memory, a theology, dozens of liturgies, precious manuscripts, and a Christian culture is preserved for many to study, adopt, and embrace.

Dale A. Johnson (Bar Yohanon)

June 2007

Brief Biography of Gertrude Bell

(1868- 1926)

Born in County Durham on July 14th 1868 to a family
of great wealth, Gertrude Bell was the daughter of the
Industrialist, Isaac Lowthian Bell. This wealth was
used to finance Gertrude's later travels around the
world. At the age of 16 Gertrude went to Lady
Margaret Hall, Oxford where she became the first
woman to achieve a first in History, after only 2 years
of study. Thereafter she traveled to countries such as
Iran, Mesopotamia, Jerusalem and Switzerland. She
developed a passion for archaeology and
mountaineering in the French Alps, (she became one
of the best female mountain climbers in the world.)
Her fascination with Arabic culture led her to learn
Arabic and associated dialects. It was rumored that
once in Jerusalem she dressed up as a man in order to
investigate the mysterious male traditions of the
Druze community.

Bell returned in 1911 to revisit the great castle at Kheidir and crossed the desert between Damascus and Baghdad. She then returned to England where she joined a movement that opposed women's suffrage. She also had an unhappy love affair with a married man.

Bell decided to return to Arabia to forget her unhappiness. This time she traveled to the city of Ha'il in the center of Arabia that had rarely been visited by Westerners. There, in 1913, Bell was held captive and robbed. When she was finally released, Arab hostility forced her to cut her journey short rather than continue to Riyadh as she had originally intended. Bell returned to Damascus in May 1914, having gained an unprecedented knowledge about the deserts of northern Arabia and the ruined cities that are found there.

In 1915 Gertrude Bell volunteered for service with the Red Cross in France but shortly after she was summoned to Cairo where she worked on behalf of the Cairo office who were helping to ferment a rebellion of the Arabs against the Turks. Because of her intricate knowledge and personal dealings with the Arab tribes Gertrude was able to offer a wealth of information that was used by T.E. Lawrence and others in the successful Arab revolt. In 1916 she arrived in Basra and was able to draw maps helping the British army reach Baghdad. Bell was the only commissioned female officer in the British army and for her work she was later awarded the C.B.E

In 1922, as the right arm of Sir Percy Cox, Britain's High Commissioner in the newly mandated Iraq, she drew the frontiers of Transjordan, Iraq, Saudi Arabia, the Yemen and adjacent territories, for her chief to present to Arab leaders at a conference at Ujair on the Gulf Coast. Churchill, Colonial Secretary in 1921, had approved her plan in outline at the Cairo Conference the year before. As Oriental Secretary in the British administration, her task was to reconcile the contradictory promises that had been made in the heat of war. When she arrived in Cairo with Cox and the Sharifian or Hashemite delegates to whom the largest of those promises was made, she was delighted to find that Churchill's package, formulated in London with the aid of the pro-Arab TE Lawrence at one elbow and the pro-Israeli Richard Meinertzhagen at the other, agreed in almost every detail with hers. Neither she nor Cox could have realized then that their attempts at reconciliation would lead to rivalries and divisions far greater and more persistent than any that had existed in the previous four centuries of Turkish rule.

Not only was Bell instrumental in first negotiating the borders of Iraq but then persuaded Churchill to accept Faisal as the new King of Iraq. Bell then acted as an adviser to Faisal, leading some to comment she was the "uncrowned Queen of Iraq" It is said Gertrude Bell and great skill in persuading politicians about her own viewpoint. Her contemporary Virginia Woolf gave this frank description of Gertrude Bell.

"a masterful woman who has everyone under her thumb, and makes you feel a little inefficient. "

Unfortunately the new nation of Iraq proved to be rather artificial leading to conflicts between different tribes. The British presence was increasingly resented and disliked leading to a long period of violent and costly confrontation. It is perhaps surprising the striking similarities to the present situation are rarely mentioned.

Known to the Arabs as Al Khatun, 'The Lady', from her pre-war travels in the desert lands, she was until her death and for a decade or more after the most famous and respected of all the Britons who had devoted themselves to the exploration and politics of the East. Her two best-known books, *The Desert and the Sown* and *Amurath to Amurath*, had long since commended her to the knowledgeable. Her letters, published posthumously by her mother, were best sellers on both sides of the Atlantic in the 1930s.

After the situation in Iraq began to be a little more stable, Gertrude was able to pursue her interest in archaeology. She founded the Baghdad Archaeology Museum with its extensive collection of artefacts dating back into antiquity and the times of Babylon. Gertrude Bell was a pioneer in calling for national treasures to be kept in the country of origin. The Baghdad Museum was one of the world's most prestigious archaeological museums.

Ten hard-working summers in the great heat of Iraq and a tribal rebellion against the new British-backed regime taxed her physically and robbed her of the will to live. Unfortunately the brilliant life of Gertrude Bell came to a tragic conclusion in July 1926. Beset by illness, and perhaps a sense of personal loneliness she took her own life with an overdose of sleeping pills.

Bell's Place in History

Not until the publication of the war adventures of her 'beloved boy', Lawrence, whom she first met at Carchemish in 1911 during his 'archaeological' period, did her star begin to wane. Nowadays, she is likely to be confused with Vanessa Bell or Gertrude Stein, or to be regarded simply as a woman explorer of exceptional merit.

Her reputation rested, like Lawrence's, on a characteristically English perception of history as a romantic legend. Her great contribution to the understanding of Arabia and its people was her observation, a quality doubtless borne in mind by her lifelong friend, David Hogarth, when he called her to serve in the Arab Bureau in Cairo during the first year of the 1914-18 war. Her descriptions of Arab chiefs and the events of the tribal territories are unsurpassed. Of King Abdal Aziz ibn Abdurrahman - or Ibn Saud as he preferred to be called - founder of modern Saudi Arabia: 'A man of splendid physique .. carrying himself with the air of one accustomed to command ..his slow sweet smile and the contemplative glance of his heavy-lidded eyes ..he combines with his qualities as a soldier that grasp of statecraft which is yet more highly prized by the tribesmen ..' She was writing, for the benefit of the Foreign Office, of a man she heartily disliked!

It has been said that her pen was dangerously alluring, particularly in terms of official report writing, a quality which perhaps owed something to her flirtation with journalism in the first decade of the century when she became the eyes and ears of The Times in lands stretching from Suez to the Tigris, under the newspaper's foreign editor Valentine Chirol, another lifelong friend and confidant. Her intelligence reports were much appreciated by successive secretaries of state at the India, Foreign and Colonial offices. In a debate before the Balfour Declaration was published, Edwin Montagu, the only Jew then in the cabinet and the minister most bitterly opposed to the offer of Palestine to the Jews, quoted Gertrude Bell's pro-Arab views to his colleagues who, though impressed, were not persuaded.

Her post-war support for the Sharifites, the family of Husain ibn Ali of Mecca, finally ensured that if they were not given the whole of the Arabian peninsula, as they were promised during the war, they would at least have Transjordan and Mesopotamia (renamed Iraq) in return for the Arab Revolt. She and Lawrence propelled Churchill to that conclusion, though she warned Lawrence to 'stop writing rot' in the press. France prevented Syria from becoming the third of the Hashemite states and Ibn Saud took the vast hinterland and the Hejaz, holy land of Islam, for himself.

The Foreign Office assistant who wrote in the 1950s that the world would be safer if Gertrude Bell and Lawrence had not been such persuasive writers may have come closer to the truth than he could have known at the time. Generals and politicians deferred to Gertrude throughout her career, sometimes to their cost.

She held the stage to the end, in a new post as director of antiquities, when Sir Leonard Woolley began the excavation of 'Ur of the Chaldees. ' Even Arab nationalists paid tribute to her dedicated work, though they often saw imperial bias where others saw Arabophilia. With an irony that would not have been lost on her, a kindly Arab gardener still puts flowers on her Baghdad grave against a background rumble of Iraqi and insurgent gunfire.

A lone woman in a man's world, she was vehemently opposed to the women's suffrage movement. But few were willing to put to the test her implicit belief that in such matters she was the exception that proved the rule.

Bell's literary accomplishments regarding Hafiz.

Among all her influential activities in the Arabic world for which she is primarily and rightly remembered Gertrude Bell also compiled one of the early English translations of the Sufi poet Hafiz, who along with

Rumi have recently become popularized in the West. On the poetry of Hafiz, Bell wrote:

"These are the utterances of a great poet, the imaginative interpreter of the heart of man; they are not of one age, or of another, but for all time"

In depicting the intensity of love, Gertrude Bell thought Hafiz comparable to the West's own Shakespeare.

"My weary heart eternal silence keeps--
I know not who has slipped into my heart;
Though I am silent, one within me weeps.
My soul shall rend the painted veil apart."

"I have estimated the influence of Reason upon Love and found that it is like that of a raindrop upon the ocean, which makes one little mark upon the water's face and disappears."

Ironically in the Victorian age a prevalent view of Islam was that it was a religion of great liberalism, even licentiousness. This was because the great Sufi poets such as Hafiz and Omar Khayyam expressed passionate love for their beloved and used terminology such as being in "drunk with the wine" In fact these were mere allegories of Divine love. Wine was a symbol of the divine ecstasy. A Tavern was the place of worship. Although Bell felt Hafiz was not only writing about mystical experiences she was able to interpret this unusual language and terms of the Sufi's and offer a sympathetic translation. This shows Bell's natural sympathy with a foreign culture and is an indication of how she was able to transcend her very British Victorian upbringing to immerse herself in a completely foreign culture. – Even a century later there are few western women who have been able to integrate so closely with the Arabic culture and people. A rare occurrence in Victorian Britain, and even rarer for a women to assimilate another very male dominated culture.

The Focus of this Book

In 1907 Bell went to Asia Minor with the British archeologist Sir William Ramsay to help excavate early Christian churches.

The two of them collaborated on a picture book of their discoveries. In 1909 she left from Aleppo in Syria and traveled through the valley of the Euphrates River to Baghdad, visiting Babylonian sites along the way. She also went to the Shi'ite holy city of Karbala. Along the way Bell was robbed of her money and, most importantly, her notebooks. The whole countryside turned out to try to find the thieves, but the objects reappeared on a rock above her camp. When the Turkish soldiers of the Ottoman government arrived, they found a nearby village deserted, the inhabitants having fled for fear of retribution. Bell blamed herself for having been careless and causing all the difficulty.

Their excavations were chronicled in *A Thousand and One Churches*.

Sir William Mitchell Ramsay (March 15, 1851 - April 20, 1939) was a Scottish writer, New Testament scholar and archaeologist. He was the first Professor of Classical Archaeology at Oxford University and pioneered the study of antiquity in what is today western Turkey.

Ramsay was born in Glasgow, Scotland, the youngest son of a third-generation lawyer, Thomas Ramsay and his wife Jane Mitchell. His father passed away when he was six years old, and the family moved from the city to the family home in the country district near Alba. The help of his older brother and maternal uncle, Andrew Mitchell, made it possible for him to have a superior education. He studied at the University of Aberdeen, where he achieved high distinction. He won a scholarship to St. John's College, Oxford, where he obtained a first class in classical moderations (1874) and in literae humaniores (1876). He also studied Sanskrit under scholar Theodor Benfey at Göttingen.

In 1880, Ramsay received an Oxford studentship for travel and research in Greece. At Smyrna, he met Sir C. W. Wilson, then British consul-general in Anatolia, who advised him on inland areas suitable for exploration. Ramsay and Wilson made two long journeys in 1881-1882. Greece and Turkey remained the focus of Ramsay's research for the remainder of his academic career. He was known for his expertise in the historic geography and topography of Asia Minor and of its political, social, cultural and religious history.

From 1885 to 1886, Ramsay held the newly created Lincoln and Merton professorship of classical archaeology and art at Oxford and became a fellow of Lincoln College. In 1886, Ramsay was appointed Regius Professor of Humanity at his alma mater, the

University of Aberdeen. He remained affiliated with Aberdeen until his retirement in 1911. In 1906, Ramsay was knighted for his scholarly achievements on the four hundredth anniversary of the founding of the University of Aberdeen.

First Visit to Tur Abin: May-June, 1909

1909: Journey to Tur Abdin

Bell began her journey in the region known as Tur Abdin in southeast Turkey in the late Spring of 1909. She recorded in her journal the following notes.

May 10-16

THE Babylonians, and after them the Nestorians and the Moslems, held that the Ark of Noah, when the waters subsided, grounded not upon the mountain of Ararat, but upon Jūdī Dāgh. To that school of thought I also belong, for I have made the pilgrimage and seen what I have seen. The snows that gleamed upon us from under the skirts of the thunderstorm when we camped at Zâkhô were the spring-time wreaths of Jebel Jûdî, and resisting all other claims, we turned our faces towards them on the following day. Selîm, the muleteer, gloried in this decision. He was a native of the hills above Killiz, and like all mountain people his spirits rose with the rising ground. Above Zâkhô the Khâbûr is spanned by a masonry bridge of four arches (Fig. 181), but when we came to Durnakh, we found the Heizil Sû innocent of bridge or ferry-boat. The river, which is the principal affluent of the Khâbûr, ran deep and swift by reason of the melting snows. In midstream its waters touched the top of my riding-boots and buffeted my mare, so that I thought she would certainly fall; indeed she would have fallen but for two of the inhabitants of Durnakh who, with garments rolled round their waists, held bravely up her chin. Another pair was attached to each of the baggage animals, the muleteers joined in the sport, and we reached the further side without loss. Four hours and a half from Zâkhô we passed by Tell Kobbîn, an ancient mound with a village of the same name a little further to the north, (Ainsworth thinks that it may mark the site of the village at which the Greeks camped on the second day from Zâkhô: *Travels in the Track*, p. 146. Xenophon mentions neither the Khâbûr nor the Heizil.) and in two hours more we entered the foothills and lunched in an oak grove near the village of Gerik. Our path led us over rising meadows to Geurmuk and Dadar, and so into the mouth of a gorge where Hasanah nestles under rocky peaks. The clouds gathered over the mountains and thunder came booming through the gorge as we pitched our tents by the edge of the stream, nine hours from Zâkhô. Hasanah is a Christian village inhabited partly by Nestorians and partly by the converts of American missionaries. The pastor of the Protestant Nestorians, if I may so call him (when I asked him what was his persuasion, he replied that he was Prôt), came at once to offer his respects, coupled with a bunch of pink roses from his garden, and I, being much attracted by his sturdy figure and simple open countenance, asked him to guide me next day through the hills. Over and above his personal charms, Kas Mattai had the advantage of a knowledge of Arabic. He spoke besides Kurdish and Syriac, but his native tongue was Fellâhî (the Peasant Language), which is no other than Assyrian. His brother Shim'ûn, who accompanied us on all our expeditions (he climbed the rocks like a cat or a

23

Grindelwalder), had nothing but Fellâhî and Kurdish and a cheerful face, but with one or the other, or all three, he made his way deep into my affections before we parted. We walked up the narrow valley, where flowers and flowering shrubs nodded over the path in an almost incredible luxuriance, and climbed the steep wooded hill-side to a point where the rock had been smoothed to receive the image of an Assyrian king, though none had been carved upon it. Above it rose a precipitous crag clothed on one side with hanging woods through which zigzagged a very ancient path, lost at times among fallen rocks and trees, while at times its embankment of stones was still clearly to be traced. On the summit of the crag were vestiges of a small fortress. The walls were indicated by heaps of unsquared stones, many of which had fallen down the hill, where they lay thickly strewn; the evidence afforded by them, and by the carefully constructed path, made it certain that we were standing upon the site of some watch-tower that had guarded the Hasanah gorge. On the opposite side rises a second crag whereon, said

HASANAH, ASSYRIAN RELIEF.

,ASSYRIAN RELIEF.

NOAH'S ARK.

Kas Mattai, are ruins of the same description. That the valley was held by the Assyrians there can be no doubt, for it is signed with their name. Below and to the west of the crag to which we had climbed there is another smoothed niche in the rock (Fig. 182), and here the work has been completed and the niche is carved with the figure of an Assyrian king, wearing a long fringed robe and carrying a sceptre. (Mr. King, who has visited Jûdî Dâgh, tells me that all the reliefs are of Sennacherib and were carved in the year 699 B.C..)

At a later age, the mountains had been occupied by Christians. Kas Mattai showed me at the foot of the crag a few vaulted chambers which he declared to be the ruins of a Nestorian monastery, and walking westward for an hour or more along the wooded ridges, we came to a second and larger monastic ruin, with a garden of fruit-trees about it, and groves of tall blue irises which had escaped from the cemetery of the monks and wandered over the hill-side.

In the high oak woods I forgot for a few hours the stifling heat which had weighed upon us ever since we had left Môsul. Each morning we had promised one another a cooler air as we neared the mountains; each evening the thermometer placed in the shade of my tent registered from 88° to 93° Fahrenheit. The heavy air was like an enveloping garment which it was impossible to cast off, and as I walked through the woods I was overmastered by a desire for the snow patches that lay upon the peaks — for one day of sharp mountain air and of freedom from the lowland plague of flies. Sefînet Nebî Nûh, the ship of the Prophet Noah, was there to serve as an excuse.

Accordingly we set out from camp at four o'clock on the following morning. Kas Mattai and Shim'ûn in their felt sandals, raishîkî, a proper footgear for the mountaineer, Selîm, whom Providence had marked out for the expedition, 'Abdu'l Mejîd, a zaptieh from Zâkhô, who had been ordained as pointedly to walk upon flat ground, and the donkey. "As for that donkey," said Fattûh, "if he stays two days in the camp eating grass. Selîm will not be able to remain upon his back." He was Selîm's mount, and Selîm, who knew his mind better than any other among us, was persuaded that he would enjoy the trip. The donkey therefore carried the lunch. We climbed for two hours and a half through oak woods and along the upper slopes of the hills under a precipitous crest. But this was not what I had come out to see, and as soon as I perceived a couloir in the rocks, I made straight for it and in a few moments stepped out upon an alp. There lay the snow wreaths; globularia nudicaulis carpeted the ground with blue, yellow ranunculus gilded the damp hollows, and pale-blue squills pushed up their heads between the stones and shivered in the keen wind. Selîm had followed me up the couloir.

"The hills are good," said he, gathering up a handful of snow, "but I do not think that the donkey will come up here, nor yet 'Abdu'l Mejîd."

We returned reluctantly to the path and walked on for another half-hour till Kas Mattai announced that the Ark of Noah was immediately above us. Among asphodel and forget-me-nots we left the zaptieh and the donkey; Selîm shouldered the lunch-bags, and we climbed the steep slopes for another half-hour. And so we came to Noah's Ark, which had run aground in a bed of scarlet tulips (Fig. 184).

There was once a famous Nestorian monastery, the Cloister of the Ark, upon the summit of Mount Jûdî, but it was destroyed by lightning in the year of Christ 766. (Ritter, Vol. XI. p. 154.)

Upon its ruins, said Kas Mattai, the Moslems had erected a shrine, and this too has fallen; but Christian, Moslem and Jew still visit the mount upon a certain day in the summer and offer their oblations to the Prophet Noah. That which they actually see is a number of roofless chambers upon the extreme summit of the hill. They are roughly built of unsquared stones, piled together without mortar, and from wall to wall are laid tree-trunks and boughs, so disposed that they may support a roofing of cloths, which is thrown over them at the time of the annual festival. To the east of these buildings there is an open court enclosed by a low stone wall. The walls both of the chambers and of the court are all, as I should judge, constructions of a recent date, and they are certainly Mohammadan, since one of the chambers contains a mihrâb niche to the south, and in the enclosing wall of the court there is a similar rough niche. Further to the west lie the ruins of a detached chamber built of very large stones, and perhaps of an earlier date. Beneath the upper rocks upon which these edifices stand, there is a tank fed by the winter snows which had not entirely disappeared from the mountain-top. Still further down, upon a small plateau, are scattered fragments of a different architecture, carefully built walls, stone doorposts, and lintels showing above the level of the soil. Here, I make little doubt, was the site of the Nestorian monastery.

The prospect from the ziyârah was as wild, as rugged and as splendid as the heart could desire, and desolate beyond measure. The ridge of Jûdî Dâgh sinks down to the north on to a rolling upland which for many miles offers ideal dwelling-places for a hardy mountain folk. There were but four villages to be seen upon it. The largest of these was Shandokh, the home of a family of Kurdish âghâs whose predatory habits account for the scantiness of the population. To the east of it lay Heshtân, which is in Arabic Thamânîn (the Eighty), so called because the eighty persons who were

28

saved from the Deluge founded there the first village of the regenerated world when they descended from Jebel Jûdî, so said Kas Mattai, but the Arab geographers would seem to place it to the south of Jûdî Dâgh, not to the north. For example, Mukaddasî says that Thamânîn, the village of the eighty who were saved from the flood, stands on the river Ghazil (the Heizil Sû), a day's march from Hasanîyeh (Zâkhô), ed. de Goeje, pp. 139 and 149. Sachau, however, speaks of Bêtmanîn as being behind Jûdî Dâgh, *i.e.* he bears out my information:*Reise*, p. 376.)

Further to the north an endless welter of mountains stretched between us and Lake Vân. They rose, towards the east, into snowy ranges, and very far to the south-east we could see the highest snow-peaks of Tiyârî, where the Nestorians, grouped under a tribal system, defend their faith with their lives against the Kurdish tribes — a hereditary warfare, marked with prodigies of valour on the part of the Christians, and with such success as the matchlock may attain over the Martini rifle.

Because the light air breathed sharply off the snows, and because the vista of mountains was a feast to the eye, we lay for several hours in the sanctuary of the Prophet Noah. There can be no manner of doubt that I ought to have completed the pilgrimage by visiting his grave, but it lay far down upon the southern slopes of Jûdî Dâgh, and I was making holiday upon the hill-tops; therefore when we turned homewards, we bade Shim'ûn conduct the donkey and 'Abdu'l Mejîd to Hasanah and ourselves kept to the crest of the ridge. Half-an-hour from the summit we met some Kurdish shepherds near a small heap of ruins, concerning which they related the following history: Once upon a time there was a holy man who took a vow of pilgrimage to the ship of Noah, and for a month he journeyed over hill and vale until he reached the spot on which we stood. And there he met the Evil One, who asked him whence he came and whither he was going. The holy man explained that he was bent on a pilgrimage to the ship of Noah. "You have still," said the Devil, "a month's journey before you." Thereat the pilgrim, being old and weary, lost heart, and since he could not return with his vow unfulfilled, he built himself a hut and ended his days within sight of the goal, if his eyes had not been too worn to see. The presence of the shepherds upon Mount Jûdî was not to be attributed to any pious purpose. They had come up from the villages below to escape from the sheep tax which was about to be levied for the second time within a twelvemonth, once for last year's arrears, and once for this year's dues. Their lawless flocks skipped among the boulders and the snow-wreaths as light-heartedly as the wild goat, which no government can assess, but the owners lived in anxiety, and when, half-an-hour further, we encountered a second company, they took us for soldiers and greeted us with rifle shots. Kas Mattai grasped the situation and shouted a justification of our existence, which was not received without hesitation. I was standing, when the shots began, in the middle of a *névé*, and thinking that I must offer a fine mark, I stepped off the snow and sat down upon a grey rock to await developments. But as soon as we had made it clear that we / were simple people with no official position, we were allowed to pass. "It was well," observed Kas Mattai, as we clambered down the crags, "that 'Abdu'l Mejîd was not with us. They would have killed him."

At the foot of the rocks we sat down to rest beside a bubbling spring.

"Have you suffered at the hand of the government?" I asked my guide.

"We suffer from the Kurds," he replied, "and there is no

one to protect us but God. Effendim, the âghâwât, and their mares, and the followers they bring with them? And how shall we refuse when they are armed with rifles?"

"Have you no arms?" said I.

"We have no money to buy rifles," he answered; "and if we bought them, the Kurds would take them from us. And when we have killed our last sheep that we may entertain them, they seize upon all we possess before they leave us."

"Oh Merciful!" ejaculated Selîm.

"Sir," said Kas Mattai, "last year they took my bed, and that which was too worthless to carry away they broke and threw upon the fire. But if we resisted they would burn the village."

We ran down through the oak woods and got into camp at four in the afternoon.

"God prolong your existence!" cried Fattûh. "Have you seen the ship of the Prophet Noah?"

"Oh Fattûh," I replied, "prepare the tea. I have seen the ship of the Prophet Noah." So it is that I subscribe in this matter to the wisdom of the Kurân: "And immediately the water abated and the decree was fulfilled and the Ark rested upon the mountain of Jûdî."

31

Next morning the camp was sent straight to Jezîreh, which it reached after a six-hours' march, but I, with Shim'ûn as guide, followed the line of the hills. We rode for two hours through the oak woods, and then crossed a gorge wherein lies the Moslem village of Evler. The incomparable beauty of these valleys passes belief. Evler was buried in a profusion of pomegranate and walnut, fig, almond and mulberry trees; the vines were wreathed from tree to tree, the ground beneath was deep in corn, and the banks of the stream aglow with oleander. An hour further we reached the Nestorian village of Shakh, where a ruined castle protects the entrance of the gorge. The walls climb up the hillside towards a citadel placed upon a high peak; above the village two deep valleys run up into the mountains, and each has been walled across, so that Shakh was guarded from attack on every side. I should judge these fortifications to be Kurdish, but there are traces of an older civilization on the rocks above them (Fig. 183). Of the four Assyrian reliefs that are reported to exist, I saw only three, the fourth being cut upon the face of the cliff and unapproachable except with ropes. Each of the three niches which I was shown (after an hour's climb in the hottest part of the day) contained a single figure, like that of Hasanah; each had been covered with cuneiform inscriptions, but in two cases both the figure and the inscriptions had all but weathered away. We left Shakh at midday, stopped for half-an-hour to lunch by the stream, and reached Jezîret ibn 'Umar at four o'clock. The camp was pitched upon a high bank overhanging the Tigris, but the bridge of boats which should have connected us with the town was broken, and I crossed by a ferry on the following day.

Diary Entries

14/05/1909

Friday May 15. [i.e. 14 May 1909] Off at 5.35. I sent my camp direct to Jezireh [Cizre] which they reached in 6 hours. Kas M. brought me roses, figs and a pomegranate. Shim'un came with me and we rode along the hill side. Oak woods of 2 kinds large and small leaved. Lovely orchises and onion things - alliums I suppose. At 7.25 we got to Evler a Moslem village in a big valley. Wonderful profusion of fruit trees - pomegranate, walnut, fig, almond, mulberry and the vine ramping over all. The corn growing beneath and oleanders in full flower. At 8.30 we reached Shakh. Just before it there is a ruined castle, a great wall climbing the hill as at Za'feran. The two valleys leading down to it are both walled across - the ruins remain. Went to Kas Sergis the Nestorian priest who accompanied us some of the way up the hill, but I sent him back because he was so much exhausted. His nephew, Shim'un came with me. We reached the first stele in 3/4 of an hour, a good deal defaced. 1/2 an hour's very steep hot climb brought us to the second which is in very good condition. Then under the crag to the third which we reached in about 1/4 of an hour. The inscrip here is almost gone. All appear to be of exactly the same type as the one above Hassana. We climbed to the summit of the crag and looked for the fourth which is somewhere on a steep face, but did not find it. Very delicious up in these rocks. Rested and cat chocolate and drank water and so back to Shakh. We left at 12; at 12.30 got down to the stream where I sat and lunched for 1/2 an hour. Then we rode over rolling ground to Jezireh which we reached at 4. The only village we passed was Zaghmur at 3. The camp was pitched on a fine high bank above the Tigris.

There is a ruin on this side opposite where the bridge was that led from the castle; it was so full of fleas that I hurried away from it. It consisted of 3 barrel vaulted chambers. Very tired.

15/05/1909

Sat May 16. [i.e. 15 May 1909] Went over to Jezireh [Cizre] at 6.15. Saw the castle which appears to be Seljuk or something of the kind. Striped black and white masonry and a little E gate with a blazon of lions. So down across the moat to the ruined bridge which is of the same style as the castle. A panel of very curious reliefs on the E side; on the W the water buttress is ornamented with a key pattern in black and white. So back to the town E gate opposite the ruined bridge over the moat. It is of the same fine masonry with a straight arch. So to the big mosque. The main doorway has a fine bronze door with lovely knockers made each one of a dragon. The inscription says [line of Arabic] no doubt An al manlana as Sultan al malih ed dunya wa ed din Abu alKasim Mahmud shahinshah. There was also a stone inscrip over the door which I cd not read but the work was not old - Persian flower patterns like those of Zakho. I looked inside but did not go in which I ought to have done for I remembered after that there was a dome and therefore a turbch. So rode back through the horrid squalid little town and ferried over. Got off at 10.15. Parted company with the caravan at 10.55 and rode over a spur into the valley of the Risur Chai. We reached the river at 11.45 and at 12 came to the Parthian sculpture, a horseman. The horse's hind leg much extended, the rider faces round, the whole thing very pseudo classical. Just above are castle ruins on both sides of the stream - half a mile above that, or less - a bridge with a ruin by it. Lovely valley leading up to the snows[?]. Full of women going up on a two day's pilgrimage to see a famous Sheikh Talib from C'ple [Istanbul (Constantinople)], so they said. We left Kasr Ghelli at 1, rode over the spurs and down to the Tigris. Thence by a very bad path to Finik. Oleanders magnificent. There is a ruined midway castle and below it rice fields and a ruin on a point by the water. Then we crossed a deep gorge full of rock cut tombs or houses (very bad road) and came to another smallish ruin on the side of the hill. A small valley followed and then another ruin a little higher up. Got into camp by the Tigris at 4. The crag castle just opposite between the two last mentioned ruins. We are camped in deep white sweet smelling clover. Made great enquiries as to Parthian sculptures. At first everyone swore there were none. At last a woman appeared from the ferry who had seen them and then everybody knew.

16/05/1909

Sunday May {17} 16. [16 May 1909] Heavy dew and quite cold in the night. I got up soon after 4 and was ready to set out at 5 but my mare needed shoeing. Finally at 5.25 I rode up to the village which lies in the rocky valley and is mostly to this day troglodyte. Extraordinarily beautiful. We got a Kurd to guide us and my soldier Hajji and I went up to the high castle, a most attractive place, much of it rock cut. The entrance gate is rock cut with ditto chambers on either side. All up the slope there are rock cut chambers and even on the summit citadel the rooms are {partly} vaulted but the walls rock cut and the stairs. I saw the remains of a rough squinch in one place. I do not think any of it is very old but some of the walls of the citadel seemed to be of finer masonry than others and there may be 2 periods. One big rock cut chamber had a niche to the S. which may have been a mihrab. So down again and across the valley to the Parthian stele. There is no water channel here (vide Ainsworth's notes to Xenophon) and no possible water conduit. He must have confused it with Kasr Ghelli where there is a rock cut conduit. I asked for Iran and my guide hurried forward and while I eat white mulberries in the village prepared me an omelet which he brought with bread and Iran. So down to the ferry at about 8 and found only one boat load had gone over. We had 2 boat loads more. The stream was very swift and when they turned the gamiyyeh into the opposite bank it as near as anything capsized - the animals all fell over. Left the ferry at 9.25. And climbed up. At 9.45 we passed the little Xian village of Handak[?]. At 10.40 Thelaila (Moslem) on the top of the plateau. The whole country smelt sweet of clover. At 12.15 we saw Kodach a little to the SE. I sat down and lunched for about half an hour. We got to Azakh (the accent is on the last syllable) at 2.15 and camped under a tree. The village is nearly all Xian. After I had visited came to see me the Khawaja Hanna and the Syrian priest (they are all Syrians here) and gave me very extraordinary news from Adana [(Seyhan, Alaniya)] and Diarbekr [Diyarbakir (Amida)]. Apparently Abd ul Hamid made a great conspiracy all over the country. The Xians are very fanatical here. They won't sell us so much as an egg because it is Sunday.

Jezîret ibn 'Umar is built upon an island formed by the Tigris and a small loop canal. It is called after a certain Hassan ibn 'Umar of the tribe of Taghlib, who lived in the ninth century.

It has been identified with the Bezabde of Ammianus Marcellinus, the Saphe of Ptolemy (ed. Mûller, p. 1005), and the Sapha of the Peutinger Tables. Ammianus Marcellinus is generally supposed to have confused Bezabde-Jezîreh with Phœnice-Finik, saying that the two names are applied to the same place. In his account of the capture of Bezabde by Sapor II, in A.D. 360, his description applies better to Finik than to Jezîreh (Bk. XX. ch. vii. I. See, however, Hartmann: *Bohtân*, Part II. p. 98). He relates further that Constantius attempted in vain to re-capture Bezabde (Bk. XX. ch. xi.), but in this passage he must mean Jezîreh. I can find little in the history of Jezîreh except the mention of sieges: by Tîmûr for example (Ritter, Vol. IX. p. 709), and by the emirs of Bohtân (Rich: *op. cit.*, Vol. I. p. 106). When Moltke visited it in 1838 it was a heap of ruins (*Briefe aus der Turkei*, Berlin, 1893, p. 251), and it was not much more when I saw it.

JEZÎRET IBN 'UMAR, GATE OF FORTRESS.

JEZÎRET IBN 'UMAR, BRIDGE.

JEZÎRET IBN 'UMAR, RELIEFS ON BRIDGE.

The castle of masonry is mostly of alternate bands of black basalt and white limestone. Over one of the doors are carved a couple of rudely executed lions. The town walls still exist in part and belong to the same date as the castle; so too does the fragment of a masonry bridge which spanned the Tigris about half-an-hour's ride below the town (Fig. 186). On our way to it we forded the moat which was at that time quite shallow. One of the bridge piers is decorated with a key pattern of black and white stone, and with some curious reliefs representing the signs of the zodiac, of which the work is similar in character to that of the lions upon the castle gate (Fig. 188). Each relief bears an inscription in Arabic naming the zodiacal sign which it depicts. Sachau notices these reliefs. In his opinion the inscriptions are of no great age. (See *Reise*, p. 379.)

As we came back through the town we stopped at the principal mosque, which has a pair of fine bronze doors, with bronze knockers worked in a design of intertwined dragons. A small dome, set upon columns that may have been taken from an earlier building, covers the fountain in the courtyard

Ibn Batûtah, in the fourteenth century, mentions an old mosque in the market place, which is probably the same as the one I saw, though it has undergone many alterations and reparations since his day.

Jezîret ibn 'Umar has a bad reputation for the fever which is bred in its marshy moat; moreover it was stifling hot. I hurried through a cursory sight-seeing and ferried back to the opposite bank, where I found the baggage animals loaded and ready to start. Having followed the Tigris bank for half-an-hour, I left the caravan to pursue its way to Finik and turned up the valley of the Risür Chai. In less than two hours from Jezîreh we came to a ruined Kurdish fort, standing on either side of the stream and blocking effectually the passage of the gorge; and carved upon the rocks of the left bank there is a more ancient guardian of the pass, a warrior armed, and mounted upon a bounding horse . His companion, who went on foot, has fallen into the stream, and I know no other record of him than Layard's woodcut.' (*See Nineveh and Babylon*, p. 55)

The figure of the horseman is much defaced by time. The winter rains have worn thin his armour, the spring floods have undermined the rock on which he stands, but shadowy though his image may be, it marks the triumph of a European civilization, and its prototypes are to be sought not among the bearded divinities and winged monsters of Assyria, but in the work of Western sculptors. The Parthian, who was the bitter enemy of the Roman empire, carved it upon the rocks of Kasr Ghelli, and bore witness with his own hand to the overmastery of Roman culture..

We cut across the hills back to the Tigris, and rode by a memorably inadequate path — equally memorable for the profusion of oleanders through which it ran — up the bank to Finik. The high ground on either side of the valley falls sharply to the water, and the river bursts here through the last barrier of mountain which divides it from the Mesopotamian plain. Finik has been from all time the key of the ravine. Before we reached the side-gorge in which the village lies, we passed a great enclosure of ruined walls and towers, and below it, among the ricefields that occupy a cape jutting into the stream, there are remains of similar fortifications. Beyond the gorge of Finik we rode under a crag which is crowned by the most commanding of the many castles, and less imposing fortress ruins are clustered about its foot. We made our way through groves of pomegranate down to the camp, pitched in clover pastures by the river. A ferry-boat was drawn up upon the bank, and with its help we designed to convey ourselves next morning to the further side, but the boat was ancient and the stream swift, and I suspected that the passage would be a long business. Therefore I left Fattûh to cope with the ferrymen.

PARTHIAN RELIEF, KASR GHELLÎ

PARTHIAN RELIEF, FINIK.

THE HILLS OF FINIK.

A tumbling stream and masses of oleander fill the gorge; the greater part of the inhabitants of Finik are lodge in caves, preserving, no doubt, the customs of their remotest ancestors whose rock-cut dwellings they have inherited.

The caves are carefully excavated and I should say that they are ancient. Layard (*Nineveh and Babylon*, p. 54) speaks of them as tombs and some may have been intended as burial-places, but I do not doubt that many were from all time used by the living. The troglodyte habits of the dwellers in these mountains are still strongly marked. Above Bâ'adrî I saw an underground village; at Hisn Keif, higher up the Tigris, the people live in rock-hewn chambers.

We climbed up to the castle by a winding path and entered it on the side furthest from the Tigris, the face of the hill turned towards the river being a precipitous rock. The castle wall is partly of masonry and partly of the natural rock, and the gate is tunnelled through the cliff and flanked by small rock-cut chambers. Within the enclosure there are a number of underground chambers, and on the highest peak the rooms are rock-hewn and vaulted with masonry. How old the rock cutting may be I cannot tell; the masonry is not very ancient, some of it may be modern, while none could safely be dated earlier than the Middle Ages. But the position overhanging the Tigris is superb, and it is difficult to think that the Phœnice which Sapor overthrew stood on any other crag. The rolling plateau of the Tûr 'Abdîn stretched away to the south-west, and since I observed that the ferrying of my caravan was taking as long a time as I had anticipated, I sat down and made a comfortable survey of the country we were about to traverse. We returned to the village by the way we had come (there is no other) and climbed the rocks on the opposite side of the valley, where Layard found a much-effaced Parthian relief. It depicts the figures of a man and a woman, clad in short tunics which hang in heavy folds over loosely-fitting trousers. Above the man's head are traces of an inscription which even in Layard's day was indecipherable. Our guide hurried back to the village while I was examining the tablet, and when we came down we found him spreading a meal of omelets and bread and bowls of irân (a most delectable drink made of sour curds beaten up in water) under the shade of some mulberry-trees — a welcome sight to those who have breakfasted early and climbed over many rocks. A less pleasing surprise awaited us when we reached the Tigris; not half the horses had crossed, and the ferry-boat was engaged in intricate and lengthy manœvres on the opposite side. There was nothing to be done but to wait for its return, and I lay down among the clover under a hawthorn-bush.

It was here that we were to bid a final farewell to the Greeks who had accompanied us from the outset of the journey. "When they had arrived at a spot where the Tigris was quite impassable from its depth and width, and where there was no passage along its banks, as the Carduchian mountains hung steep over the stream, it appeared to the generals that they must march over those mountains, for they had heard from the prisoners that if they could cross the Carduchian heights they would be able to ford the sources of the Tigris in Armenia." (*Anabasis*, Bk. IV. ch. i.)

They turned north, therefore, and fought their way through the land of the Carduchi, which are the Kurds, until they reached the sea, while we, having a ferry-boat at our disposal and a smaller force to handle, passed over the Tigris into the Tûr 'Abdîn. So at length we parted, and Cheirosophus in advance with the light-armed troops scaled the hills of Finik and led slowly forward, leaving Xenophon to bring up the rear with the heavy-armed men. Their shields and corselets glittered upon the steep, they climbed, and reached the summit of the ridge, and disappeared. . . .

"Effendim!" Fattûh broke into my meditations.

"Effendim, the boat is ready."

"Oh Fattû," said I, "the Greeks are gone."

Fattûh looked vaguely disturbed.

"The Greeks of old days, who marched with us down the Euphrates," I explained.

The history of the Ten Thousand is not included in the Aleppine curriculum, and since Fattûh can neither read nor / write, he is debarred from supplementing the acquirements of his brief school-days, but he searched his memory for fragments of my meaningless talk.

"Those?" he said. "God be with them!"

We had more reason to invoke the protection of the Almighty on our own behalf. The ferry-boat was packed with our baggage animals, standing head to tail; the current was very swift. We shot down it, heading aslant, until we neared the further shore; the ferrymen thrust their long poles sharply into the water, and the boat heeled round until the gunwale touched the level of the stream. Thereat the horses tumbled over like ninepins, one upon the other, and I, sitting high in the stern, was saved by the timely clutch of a zaptieh from plunging headlong into the stream. "Allah, Allah!" cried the ferrymen, and we ran aground upon the bank.

The Tûr 'Abdîn, which we now entered, is a lofty plateau that stretches from Finik on the east to Mardîn and Diyârbekr on the west, and south to Nisîbîn. The Tigris embraces it to north and east; on the south side the heights of the plateau fall abruptly into the Mesopotamian deserts which, interrupted only by the long hog's back of the Jebel Sinjâ, extend to the Persian Gulf. The Mount of the Servants of God — such is the meaning of its beautiful name — was known to the ancients as Masius Mons and Iazala Mons, Mount Izala occupying the eastern end of the plateau. Ammianus Marcellinus, when he speaks of Izala, evidently intends the name to cover the whole Tûr 'Abdîn. (**bk.** XVIII. ch. vi. 11, and Bk. XIX. ch. ix. 4.)

This country lay upon the confines of the Roman and the Persian empires, and in the confused accounts of the campaigns of Constantius, Justinian and Heraclius the frontier fortresses of Izala and Masius play a conspicuous part. While war raged round Amida, Marde, Dara and Nisibis, the secluded valleys of the Tûr 'Abdîn were falling peacefully into the hands of the Servants of God. The Mount was a stronghold of the Christian faith; monastery after monastery rose among the oak woods, the rolling uplands were cleared and planted with/ vineyards, and the ancient communities of the Eastern Church multiplied and grew rich in their almost inaccessible retreat. The Jacobites and the Syrians (*i.e.* Jacobites who have submitted to Rome) have now ousted the Nestorians, who must have been the first to occupy the Tûr 'Abdîn. When this change took place I do not know, but the Nestorians were in possession of the monastery of Mâr Augen as late as 1505:. (Pognon, *op. cit.*, p. 109.)

Very little has been published concerning the architectural remains of the district, but I had happened to see in Môsul some photographs which had awakened my curiosity, and the Dominican fathers whom I met at Baviân had raised it still higher. Pognon's account of the churches, and his publication of the inscriptions, is the best work on the subject (*Inscriptions de la Mêsopotamie*); Parry (*Six Months in a Syrian Monastery*) gives a short description of the churches and some sketch plans.

The morning was half spent before we landed on the west bank of the Tigris. our path climbed up on to the plateau and led us over downs sweet scented with clover and very thinly populated: during the five hours' journey from the Tigris to Azakh we saw only three villages.

Tigris ferry 9.25; Handak (Christian) 9.45; Thelailah (Moslem) 10.40; Kôdakh — marked in Kiepert — we saw at 12.15, a little to the south of our route.

Azakh, where we camped, is inhabited mainly by Jacobites, some of whom have modified their creed under the influence of American missionaries. The Protestant pastor paid me a visit and brought disquieting news. While we were still at

46

Môsul we had heard rumours of a massacre of the Christians which had taken place at Adana. The Tûr 'Abdîn was full of these reports. It was impossible to make out whether the events which were related to us were past or present, how serious the massacre had been or whether it were now at an end, and it was not until I reached Cæsarea that I learnt the truth with regard to the double outbreak in Cilicia. For a month we were greeted wherever we went with details of fresh calamities that were in part the reverberation of those of which we had already heard, and everywhere these histories were accompanied by the assurance that a deliberate attempt had been made from without to stir up massacres in the districts through which we passed. No direct proof of this statement was offered; I never met the man who had set eyes on the reported telegram, nor any one who could tell me what signature it bore. But in the East, conviction does not wait upon evidence. I learnt to realize the evil power of rumour, and experience taught me how hard it is to keep the mind steadily fixed upon the proposition that two unsupported statements (or the same often repeated) will not make a certainty. The atmosphere of panic which surrounded us is the true precursor of disaster, and I found good reason to respect the statecraft of the Turkish officials whose firmness saved the population from the consequences of their own loudly expressed suspicions. I bear testimony to the fact that all that I saw or heard of the agitation which attended the events of April 1909 led me to the conviction that the local authorities had set their face against bloodshed, and by so doing had averted it.

From Bell's Diary

17/05/1909

Monday May {18} 17. [17 May 1909] Off at 5.30 with Jusef and Reshid leaving the caravan to follow. We rode over wide uplands, in great part entirely uncultivated and covered with small oaks. It reminded me rather of the slopes leading out of the Belka towards the desert - from Gilead to Road[?]. Very little water. No streams but occasionally deep rain water pools in the valleys. At 6.30 we passed a ruined site marked in K [Kiepert]. At 7.5 the small village of Salakün (Moslem). At 8 Middeh (K. Middo) Xian, on the further side of a deep dry gorge. Then we got into the oak woods. At 9 we saw Irmez about a mile to the S. and at 9.25 'Arba also about a mile to the S. It is Xian. At 9.45 we came to the ruined Der Mar Shim'un in a valley below Ba Sabrin [Basbirin]. I stayed here till 10.35, examined it and lunched. It has no architectural interest. The church is a chapel without aisles, 2 engaged piers on either side of the nave, very high walls and a vault. The half caps of the piers are built and plastered - no decoration. To the S. of it lies a kind of vaulted narthex separating it from the central court of the monastery in which is a vaulted cistern or spring. The monastic buildings are vaulted chambers on the N., W. and S. of the court. So we rode on to Der Barsanma[?] which we reached at 11.20. Stayed there till 11.45.

It is inhabited by one young priest and distinguished by its high rather tapering rectangular tower. There is the usual central court with the cistern, rooms to the N, the tower to the E, then you enter the monastic buildings a single chamber which leads into the church which lies to the S of it.

Deir Bar Sauma

The church is again an aisleless chapel with one engaged pier on either side. Vaulted and very rudely built. (All these buildings are of rough feld steine.) Through the monastic chamber to the E you pass into other vaulted rooms, totally dark and with pools of water on the floor. So we rode up to the village of Ba Sabrin [Basbirin] and went to the small monastery of Miriam el 'Adda.

A tiny chapel to the N of the court with one engaged pier on either side, very rude, remains of rude fresco - angels; monastic chambers to the W of the court. Curious stone built book rests in the court on which the priest lays the holy books when he celebrates the feast of the monastery.

So on to the principal monastery Mar Dodo.

It is very large, surrounded by a high wall. The church lies to the N of the court with a narthex along the S side of it. The single nave has 4 engaged piers on either side. The whole building is very rude and unskilful. For instance the apse is not covered with a semi dome but with a barrel vault and the corners of the walls are roughly built in to simulate the half circle [sketch]. There is a porch over the narthex door and a stair to the left leads up to the top of it where there is an inscrip built into the wall saying that the church was built in 1510 Seleucid. But the inscrip. is modern. To the right of the porch on the E side of the court there is a big niche with a semidome. Engaged caps on either side rough Corinthian and a cross in relief carved over the semidome. The monastic chambers lie to the N, W and S. So we rode down the hill and lay under a tree waiting for the caravan, I slept. Ba Sabrin was almost destroyed 2 years ago by Kurds from Midyat way and many of the inhabitants killed. The caravan came up and we went on 3/4 of an hour through vineyards to Sare. After tea went into the village to see the Parthian(?) stele.

It is a square column, perhaps an altar(?) with an inscrip. on one side and the figure of a man on another. The other 2 sides much ruined. Found the Agha of the village, who is the chief Agha of all these parts, [space left blank], entertaining friends. Went into the church but was driven out by the fleas. It seemed however interesting. Two piers in nave with 2 barrel vaults running N and S. Then the sanctuary. The priest declared that the fleas were swept out every Sunday.

Letter to Mother

[17 May 1909]

[17 May 1909] Sunday May 17. Azakh. Dearest Mother. I seem to have done a great deal these last two days without getting along very fast. The fact is there is so much to see in all this country; I'm at it all day without end. Yesterday I began by crossing the river and looking at Jezireh [Cizre] where there is an interesting castle and a very fine ruined bridge with most curious reliefs on it - Seljuk? Kurdish? I don't know. With all this we did not get off till 10 and then I rode up into a valley to see a Parthian relief. It was a most beautiful place - I've never seen anything more exquisite than these deep rocky valleys of the Kurdish hills and at this moment they are all one rosy mass of oleanders. I found my relief; it is a horseman and it is cut in a narrow defile where the rocks come down steeply into the river. There are remains of Kurdish fortresses on either side of the stream - all very wild and splendid. So I eat my lunch under the shade of the rocks in great content and talked to processions of delightful Kurdish women who were going up the valley on a two days' journey to see a famous sheikh who lives up in the hills. We made shift to understand one another in Turkish. Then we went down to the Tigris valley and rode up it through banks of oleander to Finik where I found the camp pitched in clover meadows by the river. The rocks here are extraordinarily bold and rugged, and on every point (so it seemed to me) there is a Kurdish fortress. There were 3 at Finik. I climbed up to the highest of them early this morning - a most attractive place, half rock cut and half built. And as for Finik itself, it's a troglodyte village in a deep, splendid gorge. I should think it looked much the same when Xenophon passed this way, though the Parthians had not in his time cut the stele in the rocks above which I went up to see. I had a Kurdish guide with me who insisted on giving me a meal of sour milk, omelet and bread before I left. So I sat under mulberry trees and eat mulberries till it was ready and then we went on our way through groves of flowering pomegranates back to the Tigris where we found the baggage being ferried over. So here I took leave of the rocky Kurdish hills and parted company with Xenophon, to my great regret: we have been travelling companions since the beginning of my journey. He went north through the mountains and I have turned west onto the great plateau which is called the Tur Abdin to see monasteries. I've a notion that some of the monasteries here are as old as any monasteries in the world and I expect they are going to give me 10 days hard work.

Summary by Bell of her Diary and Letters

Next morning we rode for six hours to Bâ Sebrîna, over wide uplands almost entirely uncultivated and covered with small oak-trees. The country was so like the swelling, thinly wooded hills that lead out of the Belkâ towards the Syrian Desert that at times I could have sworn that we were riding from Gilead into Moab.[1]

Our itinerary was as follows: 5.30 Azakh; 6.30 a ruined site (marked in Kiepert); 7.5 Salakûn (Kiepert: Salekon Kharabe), a small Moslem village; 8 Middo (marked in Kiepert), a Christian village on the further side of a deep gorge (here we got into the oak woods); 9 Irmez, about a mile to the south of our road; 9.25 Arba', a Christian village also about a mile south; 9.45-10.45 Deir Mâr Shim'ûn, a ruined monastery;

11.30 Deir Bar Sauma, the first monastery of Bâ Sebrîna.

The characteristic feature of the Tûr 'Abdîn is the absence of streams; even when we crossed a deep valley, as we did twice during the course of the morning, there was no running water in it. The water supply of the villages is derived from pools which are fed by the winter rains and snows. In the second valley we found the ruined monastery of Mâr Shim'ûn, placed among thickets and deep herbage, but, to my disappointment, it was of little architectural interest. The village of Bâ Sebrîna is wholly Christian. it has been an important place and though it has now fallen to the estate of a small hamlet, it contains innumerable monasteries. Several of these are beyond the limits of the town. They lie, each in its own enclosing wall, like small forts upon the hills, and each is garrisoned by a single monk. The monastic buildings are exiguous, and I doubt whether they can have been intended for more than one or two persons; perhaps they should be regarded as clerical rather than as monastic foundations. (Monasteria clericorum. See *The Thousand and One Churches*, p. 461.) and the living-rooms were intended for the lodging of those who served the shrine. The first monastery which we reached upon the outskirts of Bâ Sebrîna was of this character. Its high and rather tapering rectangular tower, and strong walls, gave it from afar a striking appearance, but the vaulted chapel and the rooms set round a tiny court were rudely built of undressed stones, almost totally dark, and devoid of decorative features. I looked at several of the monastic houses within the village, and always with the same results: they had no pretension to architectural interest and were without ornament or inscriptions by which to determine their date. But at the monastery of Mâr Dodo I found a clue to the history of Bâ Sebrîna. The church, which is the largest in the place, stands upon the north side of a walled court round which are placed insignificant living-rooms, store-rooms and stables. The church consists of a closed narthex running along the south side of a vaulted aisleless nave, with a single apse to the east. On the east side of the court, south of the church, there is an exedra covered by a semi-dome and provided with a stone reading-desk on which to set the holy books. All the masonry is rude and unskilful, and the carved capitals and moulded arch of the exedra bear no sign of great antiquity, while the engaged capitals in the church are merely blocked out. Now this scheme of a single-chambered church, with a narthex to the south and an external exedra, filled me with amazement, for it was unlike any that I had seen, but I was subsequently to learn that it is one of the oldest ecclesiastical plans of the Tûr 'Abdîn, and its combination at Bâ Sebrîna with rough masonry and late decorative details is explained by a Syriac inscription above the porch which states that the church was built in the year 1510 of the Seleucid era, *i.e.* A.D. 1200. Whether this be the date of the first foundation or of a fundamental reconstruction upon an older site I cannot be certain, though from the absence of all trace of early work I incline to the former alternative, and I conclude that the old architectural scheme of the Tûr 'Abdîn was adhered to closely at a later date, when a second period of building activity saw the foundation of the churches and monasteries of Bâ Sebrîna. But since I did not then know that these edifices were exact copies of more ancient work, their recent date was a rude shock, and I began to wonder whether the Mount would prove to be as fruitful a field as I had hoped. Bâ Sebrîna, at any rate, had been drawn blank, and we rode down for three-quarters of an hour through vineyards to the village of Sâreh. As soon as we had settled upon a camping-ground — no easy matter on account of the interminable vineyards — I walked down to the village to examine the church. The âghâ of Sâreh belongs to one of the leading Kurdish families of these parts. I found him in an open space near the church, entertaining friends who had ridden over from a neighbouring village. They too were âghâs of a noble house, and they were tricked out in all the finery which their birth warranted. Their short jackets were covered

56

with embroidery, silver-mounted daggers were stuck into their girdles, and upon their heads they wore immense erections of white felt, wrapped round with a silken handkerchief of which the ends stuck out like wings over their foreheads. They pressed me to accept several tame partridges which they kept to lure the wild birds, and while we waited for the priest to bring the key of the church, they exhibited the very curious stela which stands upside down in the courtyard. (Pognon: *op. cit.*, p.108. the stela has not, as Pognon feared, been destroyed. The script is in an unknown alphabet, which Pognon believes/to be the prototype of Pehlevî. He gives excellent photographs of the two inscriptions; my photograph shows the relief on the third side. The fourth side is much weather-worn.)

Meantime the village priest had arrived, and I followed him unsuspiciously into the church. But I had not stood for more than a minute inside the building than I happened to look down on to the floor and perceived it to be black with fleas. I made a hasty exit, tore off my stockings and plunged them into a tank of water, which offered the safest remedy in this emergency.

"There are," said the priest apologetically, "a great many, but they are all swept out on Sunday morning. On Sunday there are none."

I confess to a deep scepticism on this head.

Diary

18/05/1909

Tuesday May {19} 18. [18 May 1909] Off at 5.30, but it was 6 before I left the village with a guide, Reshid and Jusef. We rode through endless oakwood without seeing a soul. My guide said there was a ruined church at one point on the hills. At 8.10 we came to a ruined village called Gernashasur and here we left the path and plunged down a deep valley which brought us at 9.15 to the jibb[?] below the castle of Hatem Tai. I climbed up with my guide. There are two lines of wall, the lower with small round buttresses in it. In the centre of all is the citadel with a very large bir which has been vaulted. In the citadel is a chamber with an apse to the E and a niche in it that looks uncommonly like a chapel. The apse is very finely built. The place has been rebuilt several times and the masonry is of all kinds. I guess it was Byz. and then Yezidi. There is a fragment of Arab inscrip. (Yezidi?) built into one gateway and bits of moulding set face downwards. I noticed too a vault partly of bricks laid slanting against the mur 6.40 at the village of Badibbe. I mounted our poor guide and walked on myself through the darkening oakwoods by a shallow solitary valley. Got into de tete. Lots of small rock cut cisterns for water or corn more likely. So down to the little troglodyte village of Gelieh Kalaki (in Arabic Mugharat Kala'ah) partly Islam and partly Yezid. One of the latter gave us milk and bread and wanted to kill a sheep for us. We left at 10.30 and rode down the valley. Among the oak woods was a Yezidi ziarah. Our Yezidi host kissed a specially big oak which we passed on the way to it and explained that they cd not take the honey out of another oak because it belonged to the shrine. Down the endless bare valley to the plain where the peasants were harvesting. At 12.30 we passed Keui Ilka on the left and at 12.50 came to Kinnik where I lunched under some trees till 1.20. We tried to find someone to shoe Jusef's horse but they said the baitar was dead and there was not a nail in the village. The priest's wife, a nice woman looking like an English parson's wife mutatis mutandis came down and made me welcome. The whole plain strewn over with mound villages and bounded by the Jebel Sinjar [Sinjar, Jabal]. So we went on through some corn and at last I insisted on leaving the path and we climbed up the stony lower slopes seamed with many valleys, Kal'at Jedid standing up ahead in its deep gorge. We met some people who told us that Usedere was still very far off which made me suspect I must be wrong in thinking that it lay at the head of the valley. So up at last into the shadow and under Kal'at Jedid most splendidly placed on crags with a double wall. We stopped to drink and eat an egg (all that was left of our food) at the big deep cistern below it and went off at 5.30. Walked up the gorge through oak woods and came out at Usedere at 7.30 and found the camp.

Summary

The incompleteness of the maps and the absence of trustworthy information led us far astray upon the following day. I had heard of a very ancient monastery that lay upon the outer edge of the Tûr 'Abdîn: upon the way thither I proposed to visit the castle of Hâtim Tâi. Accordingly I spread out Kiepert, and drawing a bee-line across the blank paper, told Fattûh to take the camp to Useh Dereh (Kiepert calls it Useden), and provided him with a zaptieh and a guide. Another villager accompanied Jûsef and me and the second zaptieh, and undertook to guide us via the castle to Useh

Dereh. We set forth from Sâreh at 5.30 and rode through uninhabited oak woods till 8.10, when we reached a ruined village from which we could see the castle of Hâtim Tâi standing up boldly on the opposite side of a deep valley. There was no road by which to reach it — not so much as a bridle path. We struggled down through the woods, dragging our horses over rocks and fallen trees, and by the special mercy of Providence reached at 9.15, and without accident, the foot of the castle hill. A path led round it to the Yezîdî village of Gelîyeh, and thither I sent Jûsef and the zaptieh with the horses, while the man of Sâreh climbed the hill with me. Hâtim Tâi was a renowned sheikh of the Arab tribe of the Tâi, but the castle which is called after him has a far longer history. The summit of the hill is enclosed in a

STELA
AT SÂREH.

I KAL'AT HÂTIM TÂI, CHAPEL.

double line of fortification following the contours of the slopes. The lower ring is provided with towers at the angles of the wall, and with round bastions of very slight projection. Within the inner enclosure stands the citadel, now completely ruined and bearing evidences of frequent reconstruction. The oldest parts are unmistakably of Byzantine masonry, and contain a chapel of which the apse is well preserved. The castle must have been rebuilt during the Mohammadan period, and then again rebuilt, for in one of the walls of the citadel there is a fragment of an Arabic inscription, which is not in its original position, neither is the inscription complete. I sent the photograph to Professor van Berchem. The inscription is merely a date: 630 (=A.D. 1232-3), or possibly 639.

The Yezîdîz declare that the castle was one of their strongholds until it passed into the hands of the Tâi, and this might account for a reconstruction of the citadel at a late period. The only other inscription which I could find is also

Arabic. It is apparently a name, with no date or further qualification, cut upon the main gate of the outer wall.

In the space between the two walls there are a number of small rock-hewn cisterns, some of which were probably intended to hold corn and other provisions. The main water supply was drawn from the large cistern in the citadel. So far as I could judge, the ruins, therefore, exhibit Yezîdî or Arab work (or both) upon Byzantine foundations, and I think it exceedingly likely that the castle of Hâtim Tâi is that Rhabdium which, according to Procopius, was fortified by Justinian. It lay, says he, on a steep rock upon the frontiers of the Roman and the Persian empires, two days from Dara. Below it was the Ager Romanorum, which has been identified with the plain between Môsul and the Tûr 'Abdîn. Since there was no water near it (there is none, as I have said, in the Tûr 'Abdîn), Justinian was obliged to cut a number of cisterns. (*The Buildings of Justinian* (Palestine Pilgrims' Text Society, p. 51.)

The whole of this description exactly fits the castle of Hâtim Tâi, and the presence of Byzantine masonry among the ruins is strongly in favour of the identification. The position of the fortress is exceedingly fine. The hills drop down sharply from its very walls into the Mesopotamian plain, where the long line of the Jebel Sinjâr, a mountain occupied almost exclusively by the Yezîdîs, alone breaks the desolate expanse.

A cruel disillusion awaited us when we reached the valley. The Yezîdîs, who were feasting Jûsef and the zaptieh on bread and bowls of milk, declared that there was no getting to Useh Dereh except by taking the path down into the plain and climbing up into the hills again by a pass at Kal'at ej Jedîd. Even the direction from which we had come was blocked to us, for we refused to contemplate a return through the woods down which we had pushed our way with so much difficulty. The Yezîdîs, who had heard from Jûsef that we had recently visited 'Alî Beg, begged us to stay the night in their caves (the village of Gelîyeh is all underground), and offered to kill a sheep for us, and when I was obliged to decline this eagerly proffered hospitality, one of their number accompanied us for some distance to show us the way. Riding through oak woods where the bees had hived in every hollow trunk we came to a small and dilapidated Yezîdî shrine, where my guide paused to kiss the largest of the trees. "It belongs to the ziyârah," he said in answer to my question. "We do not collect the honey out of any of these trees; all the wood here belongs to the ziyârah." We left Gelîyeh at 10.30 and in two hours found ourselves in the familiar Mesopotamian landscape, an interminable flat strewn with big mounds, each with its village near it. The climate, too, was familiar, and we rode wearily through a burning heat to which we had not thought to return. At 11.30 we passed near Kalka; at 12.30 we came to Kinik, where we spent half-an-hour trying to re-shoe one of our horses. But the farrier was dead, so we were informed, and though we had the shoe with us the whole village could not produce a single nail. When once the Yezîdî was gone none of our party had any special knowledge of the way, but Kiepert (upon whom be praise!) served us well, and with his help we hit off the valley which led up to Kal'at ej Jedîd, and at five o'clock we found ourselves, tired and hungry, under its towers. It soared above us, no less splendidly placed than Kal'at Hâtim Tâi, and guarded this second pass just as Hâtim Tâi had guarded the other. If we had been certain that we should reach our camp before nightfall I should have climbed up to it, but in the mountains no one can make a sure calculation of distances, and we dared not stay. I know nothing, therefore, of Kal'at ej Jedîd but its magnificent outer aspect, and it remains in my memory as a vision of wall and tower and precipitous rock rising into the ruddy sunset light above a shadowy gorge, a citadel as bold and menacing as any that I have seen. I would suggest that

Kal'at ej Jedîd may occupy the site of the Sisaurana of Procopius, which was destroyed by Belisarius. Sisaurana, however, lay three miles from Rhabdium, and even as the crow flies the distance between K. Hâtim Tâi and K. ej Jedîd must be greater. But the important position of K. ej Jedîd on one of the few passes up from the plain suggests that the spot must have been fortified in ancient times. Sisaurana is no doubt the Sisara of Ammianus Marcellinus. (see Ritter, Vol. XI. p. 150 and pp. 400-401.)

Letter to Family

Wed May 20. [20 May 1909]

Wed May 20. [20 May 1909] We had a tremendous day yesterday, not very profitable archaeologically but unforgettable in itself. We set off with a guide from Sare at 6 in the morning and rode for 2 hours and more through oak woods, up and down valleys entirely and absolutely desolate by narrow little rocky paths. And at last we came to a hill top from which we saw in front of us, across a deep valley, the great castle of Hatem Tai which commands the gorge leading up from the Mesopotamian plain. There was no road to it unless we went miles round, which I was determined not to do, so we struggled down the hillside, the horses hopping as best they might over rocks and trees, and got to the foot of the castle hill without mishap. I climbed up with my guide; it was a splendid place, with 2 lines of wall and a citadel on top of all, Byzantine, I should think, in the beginning - one of the outposts of the empire - and then probably a Yezidi stronghold. We came down into a troglodyte

Yezidi village where the people gave us bread and sour curds and were very anxious, when they heard I had visited Ali Beg, to kill a sheep for me. And now came a grave disillusion: there was no road through the hills to the place to which I had sent my camp and if we wanted to get there we had to go down into Mesopotamia and up again by another pass. The country is unmapped and in mountains who can tell what difficulties may lie ahead. There was nothing else for it, so we set off at 10.30 and toiled down the rocky valley into the plain and then for hours across the low ground, until at last I made out which was the pass we were heading for and turned up over the pathless foothills towards it, to the great disgust of my soldier and my guide. This determination was justified by the events, there was nothing impassible between us and the gorge and at 5.30 we found ourselves at the foot of another great crag-built castle guarding the second pass. There was no time to climb up to [it], for Heaven alone knew how far the winding mountain paths might yet take us; it remains for me a vision of tower and wall and preciptious rock lifting itself up into the sunlight above a dark gorge full of shadow - a citadel more stern and menacing that any I have ever seen. So we climbed up and up, walking now for our poor horses had done about as much as they could, and a little before 7 we found ourselves once more at the top of the hills, but a long way still from our camp. I left the men to bring the horses along and plunged down through the silent oak woods, on and on through shallow winding valleys where there was never a soul to be seen, and just as I was beginning to feel that I must be walking in a dream, and that nothing would ever put an end to the oak woods and the winding rocky path, the valley opened and there was my camp. I got in at 7.30. But it is bewitched this country; today we rode for 2 hours through the oak woods and found ourselves in the 4th century AD. Just over the lip of the rocky hills, with all Mesopotamia spread out before it, lies the mother monastery of all this country - it was founded by St Eugenius (Augen) who was a disciple of St Anthony, and the rule he instituted holds good to this day.

I have never yet seen one of the earliest monasteries still inhabited. There are 10 monks who live in caves hollowed out of the rock; they eat nothing but bread and lentils and oil and some may see no women, so that they had to lock themselves up in their caves while I was planning the church. The prior made a special exception for me (since, as he explained, very few travellers came that way); not only did he show me all over the monastery and climb with me into the cave-cell of St Eugenius, but he prepared me a lunch of omelet, lentils and raisins (the monastery kitchen is a big cave) and served it for me in his own cell, which is also a cave. High up in the rock, almost unapproachable except by a very athletic climber, lives an old bishop. He has taken a vow of silence, his food is hoisted up by him once a day in a basket, and when his last mortal sickness comes upon him he will send down word (in the basket) that he is about to die and they may come up to fetch his body. The prior was a young man of about 30; he proposes to spend the rest of his life in the monastery and in due time I suppose that he in turn will mount to the bishop's cave. They say the church is 4th century; the greater part of it certainly can't be later than 6th century, I judge, and I don't doubt that the cell of St Eugenius is authentic; so here you have the earliest hermit ideal of monasticism going on uninterrupted and unchanged until today. Half an hour away across the hills is another monastery founded by a disciple of St Eugenius, not quite so interesting, but still very wonderful. Like the first it lay on the steep mountain side, the walls climbing up almost to the top of the hills. There was a bishop here too - they seem to be plentiful - but though he is not quite so exclusive as the other bishop he was too exclusive to wish to see me. Perhaps you wonder why a monk from Egypt should have come so far. I know why: it was because Iris Sasiana grows wild among the rocks. The great grey flowers lift themselves up in masses in the open spaces between the oak bushes, gleaming silver in the strong sun, so perfect in form and so exquisitely delicate in texture that you hold your breath in wonder. I looked at them, too, with despair, for they won't throw up one littlest flower on our rock garden, do what I will. I shall have to come and live here in a cave every spring.

Summary from Bell's Book

We led our horses up the rugged gorge, and at 6.40 regained the plateau of the Tûr 'Abdîn. A little village, Bâ Dibbeh, stood at the head of the pass, and before us stretched a rolling, thickly wooded country. We stopped at the village pool to inquire our way, and were given the general direction of Useh Dereh, coupled with a vague assurance that it was not far. The paths were too stony for riding, and to walk was a relief after so many hours of the saddle; I left my companions to bring on the horses and turned into the darkening oak woods. For close upon an hour I followed the course of a shallow winding valley; the trees, standing close about the path, obscured all view; a brooking silence, unbroken by man or beast, hung over the forest, the dark deepened into cool, sweet-smelling night, and still the narrow rocky path wound on between wooded banks. And just as I was wondering whether it had any end, the trees fell back round an open patch of corn and vine, and the lights of my camp shone out upon the further side.

If we had travelled far in the body upon that day, we travelled further in the spirit upon the next. There lies upon the lip of the hills, overlooking the wide desolation of Mesopotamia, a monastery which is said to be the mother house of all the Tûr 'Abdîn. Into these solitudes, according to the tradition of the mountain, wandered at the beginning of the fourth century a pupil of St. Antony, whose name was St. Eugenius. He had learnt from his master the rule of solitude and had overcome with him the devils that people the Egyptian sands; among the rocks of Mount Izala he laid down his pilgrim's staff, gathered disciples about him and founded the monastery that still bears his name. It was at first no more than a group of cells hollowed out of the cliff, but as its fame increased, the monks built themselves a church upon a narrow shelf between precipice and precipice, and helped

68

out the natural defences of the mountain by a strong wall of masonry. The cave cells increased in number until the rocks were honeycombed on every side, and disciples of the first founder led forth companies of monks to raise fresh monasteries over the Tûr 'Abdîn. Though tradition links these foundations with Egypt, it is quite possible that they may have had a yet closer connection with Syria, where in the fourth century monasticism and the solitary life had already taken a strong hold. (Duchesne: *Histoire de l'Eglise*, Vol. II. p. 516.)

The Jacobite priest of Useh Dereh, when he heard that we proposed to visit Mâr Augen, offered to accompany us, saying that he wished to pay his respects to the bishop who lived there (this was a figure of speech, for the bishop is not to be seen of any man), and he guided us for an hour through the woods to the southern edge of the hills. Kiepert marks a "Gr. Cænobium van Izala," which is, I imagine, intended for Mâr Augen, but its position relatively to K. ej Jedîd and Useh Dereh, as marked in the map, cannot be correct. Mâr Yuhannâ, which lies to the east of Mâr Augen, approaches more nearly to Kiepert's site. I have published a short account of these and other monasteries and churches of the Tûr 'Abdîn in *Amida* (Strzygowski and Van Berchem).

The path to the monastery was a rock-cut staircase, but we succeeded in dragging the horses down it and left them by the gate. Under the crag stands the church with its tiny cloister and walled court, and it did not take long to discover that, in spite of many rebuildings, the tradition as to its age could not be far wrong. A church must have stood here in the sixth century, if not in the fifth; some of the old capitals have been re-used at a later time, and the ancient plan is preserved in church and cloister. Ten monks are lodged in the rock-cut cells of their remote forerunners—I met with one of them in the cloister and he carried intelligence of my arrival to the prior, who came in haste to do the honours of his church. He was a man of some thirty years of age, with melancholy eyes. We sat together in the shadow of the cloister, while he explained to me the rule under which he and his brethren lived, and as he spoke I felt the centuries drop away and disclose the ascetic life of the early Christian world. They spend their days in meditation; their diet is bread and oil and lentils; no meat, and neither milk nor eggs may pass their lips; they may see no woman—

"But may you see me?" I asked.

"We have made an exception for you," explained the prior. "Travellers come here so seldom. But some of the monks have shut themselves into their cells until you go."

The cell of St. Eugenius stands apart from the others, hollowed out of the cliff to the west of the church. The prior had spent a lonely winter there, seeing no one but the brother who brought him his daily meal of bread and lentils. As we stood in the narrow cave, which was more like a tomb than a dwelling-place. , I looked into the young face, marked with the lines drawn by solitude and hunger.

"Where is your home?" I asked.

"In Mardîn," he answered. "My father and my mother live there yet."

"Will you see them again?" said I.

"Perhaps not," he replied, but there was no regret in his voice.

"And all your days you will live here?" He looked out calmly over rock and plain. "Please God," he said. "It seems to be a good place for prayer."

It is the habit of the monks to let no traveller depart without food, a habit well known to the neighbouring Kurds who claim more hospitality than the monastery can well afford. While I worked at the church, the prior betook himself to the cave kitchen and prepared an ample meal of eggs and bread, raisins and sour curds for me and for my men. When we had eaten I asked whether it would not be seemly to thank the bishop for the entertainment which had been offered to us.

"You cannot see him," said the prior. "He has left the world."

"The kas from Useh Dereh came to-day to visit him," I objected.

"He came to gaze upon his cell," answered the prior, and with that he led me out of the church and pointed to a cave some fifty feet above us in the cliff. Three-quarters of the opening had been filled with masonry, and I could see that it was approached by a stair of which the lower part was cut out behind a gallery and the upper on the face of the rock. An active novice might have thought twice before attempting the path to the bishop's cell.

"Is he old?" said I.

"He is the father of eighty years," replied the prior, "and it is now a year since he took a vow of silence and renounced the world. Once a day, at sunset, he lets down a basket on a rope and we place therein a small portion of bread."
"And when he dies?" I asked.

"When he is sick to death he will send down a written word telling us to come up on the next day and fetch his body. Then we shall see his face again."

"And you will take his place?" said I.

"If God wills," he answered.

We walked across the hills for half-an-hour to Mâr Yuhannâ, a monastery founded by a disciple of St. Eugenius. It is neither so finely placed nor so interesting architecturally as Mâr Augen, though the rough walls of church and monastic building, which cling to the rocky slopes are not without a certain wild beauty. The bishop who rules over the house of Mâr Yuhannâ is less exclusive than the prelate at Mâr Augen, for he shares a tower with his four monks, but he was still too exclusive to receive my visit. The aged prior was all for serving us with a meal, but I could not undertake to dispose of another omelet, nor did I realize that my refusal would be regarded as a shocking breach of the social code. The prior was so deeply hurt that he would not bid us farewell, and we left under the cloud of his displeasure. We climbed back to the summit of the hills and rode home to

Useh Dereh, and if any one should wonder why a recluse from Egypt should have sought so distant a dwelling-place as Mount Izala, I can give a sufficient answer. It was because he found Iris Susiana growing among the rocks. The great grey flowers lift their heads in every open space between the oak-trees, gleaming silver in the strong sun, and so perfect are they in form, so exquisite in texture, that I stood amazed at the sight of them, as one who gazes on a celestial vision.

Diary Entry

19/05/1909

Wed May {20} 19. [19 May 1909] Left at 6 and rode up through the oak woods to Der Mar Augen.

just over the lip of the hills. Iris Susiana in flower in the woods, most lovely. Mar Augen is the mother house of this district. We got to it after about 2 hours succeeding in pulling our horses down over the rocks. There are 10 monks; they live mostly in caves some of which have upper chambers. I do not doubt that this is the real primitive monasticism. The bp, an old man, has shut himself up in a cave, walled in and almost inaccessible above the monastery and intends to spend the rest of his days in silence. He eats once a day; the food is hoisted[?] up to him in a basket - burghul, bread, lentils and oil - none of the monks eat anything else. The rais entertained me and told me how they were oppressed by the Kurds. He took me up to Mar Augen's cell in the rocks above the monastery to the W. The kitchen is a half open cave with a big cave behind it as storehouse - skins of burghul in it. Several of the monks wd not look at a woman and were carefully sent into their caves. The rais made an exception in my favour. The monastery owns lands and vinyards [sic] but only so much of the produce is assigned to it by the church at large as is necessary for the livelihood of the monks. Rather heated discussion as to whether all Moslems go to Hell, a propos of the Sultan! The Rais gave me lunch in his cell, omelet, burghul and raisins. He proposes, if allowed, to spend the rest of his days at Mar Augen. His native place is Mardin. We sent the horses up to the wine press which we had passed in the woods on our way (it was for dibs the Kas of Usedere said) and walked on over the hills to Mar Yuhanna about 1/2 an hour away.

Less interesting but the same brick arches in the
sanctuary and bricks used in the high vault. The door
arch between ante chamber and nave set back, the
arches over the niches in the anti chamber wall set
forward. The anti chamber covered with a fine brick
dome on squinches. There is a modern (I think) small

chapel below the church. In the N wall of the church is the tomb of Mar Yuhanna and that of his mother in the S. wall. There are 4 monks here; also a bp. They live in a sort of tower and caves at the very top of all. We offended the old rais mortally by refusing to eat. So back to the dibs press. There are 2 caves and in front of one a number of rock cut cavities with rock cut channels for the dibs to run out of the cave into the cavities. So home and into camp at 4. It is just an hour's ride from Useh Dereh to Mâr Melko,

Summary by Bell of Monasteries of Tur Abdin

Kiepert places Mâr Melko too far from Useh Dereh. My itinerary was as follows: Useh Dereh to Mâr Melko, 1 hr.; Mâr Melko to Kharabah 'Aleh, 30 min.; Kharabah 'Aleh to Kernaz, 2 hrs. 15 min.; Kernaz to Deir el 'Amr, 1 hr. 15 min. All these places are marked in the map.

The bishop (for there was a bishop here also—the number of prelates in the Tûr 'Abdîn is scarcely to be reckoned) was singularly unlike his colleagues of the other monasteries. He carried sociability to so high a point that I doubted whether I should be allowed to proceed that day upon my journey, but with the regrettable incident at Mâr Yuhannâ fresh in my memory, I put force upon my appetite and ate the second breakfast upon which his hospitality insisted, while the zaptieh and Jûsef, who were not in the habit of counting breakfasts, did fuller justice to the remains of it. The monastery is a rambling building with a chapel upon an upper floor and a crypt containing the tombs of priors. The tomb of the patron saint is in the church itself. Over it hangs a rude picture of Mâr Melko with the devil beside him: upon inquiry the bishop explained that the saint had been renowned for his power of casting out devils, and he pointed to a collar and chain attached to the wall and observed that men who were afflicted with fits or madness came here to be cured, and all went away sound, no matter what their creed. Niebuhr heard that Mâr Melko was famed for the curing of epilepsy: *Reisebericht*, Vol. II. p. 388. Not having penetrated into the Tûr 'Abdîn, he thought that the report that there were seventy monasteries in the hills must be an exaggeration, but I expect that it was not far from the truth.

The buildings bore evidences of frequent reconstruction, and parts of the church were still in the state of ruin in which a recent Kurdish raid had left them. It is almost impossible to date architecture of this kind, for the new work and the old have much the same character, but the plan of the church is the ancient monastic scheme, as I learnt at Mâr Gabriel and at Salâh, and in all probability Mâr Melko is to be counted among the oldest foundations of the Tûr 'Abdîn. Like Mâr Gabriel it is some distance removed from the nearest village, and depends for its security upon its own strong walls. After we had passed through Kharabah 'Aleh, which contains the ruins of a church, we wandered among the rolling, wooded hills, and had gone needlessly far to the north before we caught sight of the monastery of Mâr Gabriel standing upon an eminence, with my tents pitched beside it. The inevitable bishop was away and I could not regret his absence, since it implied a relaxation of the social duties which I should otherwise have been obliged to fulfill, and permitted me to give my whole attention to the building.

Letter by Bell to Family

20/05/1909

Thurs May {21} 20. [20 May 1909] Off at 5.30. It was just an hour's ride to Mar Melko

and we stayed till 7.45. It stands up square on its hill and has a very fortress like air. The bp here was very cordial but rather an old bore. He was not at all satisfied with my mejideh bakhshish. Impossible to plan the monastery as it goes up and down everywhere. Below the church[?] (you reach it by a door in the court, below and W of the church) is a crypt with graves. No architectural interest. The bp has 3 monks here. So we rode on but as Reshid did not know the way Heaven knows where we went. At 8.15 we reached a village called Kharabe 'Ale. There we went wrong. At 10.30 we passed a tiny village called Chevnos; there were some houses on the hill top above it. At last at 11.45 we got onto a hill and saw Der el Amer (Mot Gabriel Monastery) in the distance. I lunched for half an hour and we got into camp at 12.50. The baggage had arrived 11/2 hours before. Spent the rest of the day planning the monastery.

The apse of the big church has a mosaic pavement - big roughly laid stones - and a mosaic roof, a cross in the centre with circles this way [sketch: figure of eight shape] apparently vine scrolls on a gold ground. Very dark and difficult to see. The bp was away. One monk and one nun were there. There are 4 monks altogether. The main altar of the big church stands under a painted wood canopy. At Mar Melko there was a picture of the saint with the devil near him just over his tomb in the nave. He cast the devil out of somebody - a king's son I think. In the further corner a chain and collar for mad people of all religions - [ag1]they all get well! Temp 90 when I got into camp though it was a cool day.

Visit to Mor Gabriel, May 20, 1909

The house of St. Gabriel of Kartmîn was, during the Middle Ages, the most famous and the richest of Jacobite establishments. It is said to have been founded in the reign of Arcadius (395-408) and rebuilt under Anastasius (491-518), and I see no reason to doubt that the great church of Mâr Gabriel is, as it now stands, a work of the early sixth century. There are two other churches within the existing monastic precincts, one dedicated to the Virgin, the other to the Forty Martyrs, but neither of these is as old as that which is dedicated to the tutelary saint. A large area of ruins beyond the walls gives some indication of the former magnificence of the monastery which gained, as early as the days of Justinian, a reputation for holiness second only

THE BISHOP OF MÂR MELKO

KHÂKH, THE NUN.

KHÂKH, CHURCH OF THE VIRGIN.

to Jerusalem. It bore at that period the name of St. Stephen; St. Gabriel was bishop of the monastery during the reign of Heraclius. When the Arab invaders drove out the forces of the Byzantine empire, he obtained from the Khalif 'Umar ibn u'l Khattâb rights of jurisdiction over all Christians in the Tûr 'Abdîn, for which reason the monastery is sometimes called after him, Deir Mâr Gabriel, and sometimes after the khalif, Deir 'Umar. It was despoiled by Timûr towards the close of the fourteenth century, and many a harrying it must have endured from the Kurds before it sank into its present state of poverty and decay. One monk and a single nun, well stricken in years, were its sole occupants at the time of my visit. The

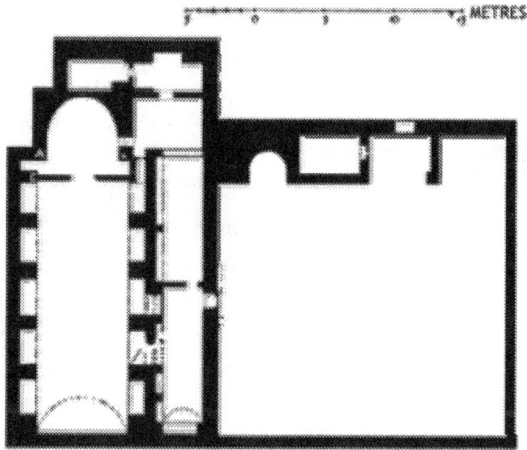

KEFR ZEH, MÂR 'AZÎZÎYEH; PARISH CHURCH.

church of Mâr Gabriel is built upon a plan which I conjecture to be monastic as distinguished from parochial. The two types, which are quite unlike each other, are also unlike all churches known to me outside the Tûr 'Abdîn. The parish church (Fig. 198), which has no domestic buildings attached to it, or nothing but a few chambers for the lodging of clerks, follows invariably the plan that I have described at Bâ Sebrina; at Mâr Gabriel, and in the other monastic churches (Fig. 199), the atrium and narthex lie to the west, the vaulted nave is placed with its greater length running from north to south, and three doors in the east wall communicate with a triple sanctuary. From what prototypes did the Christian architects of the Tûr 'Abdîn derive the singular feature of the nave lying with its greater length at right angles to the main axis of the building? I can only suggest that they may have preserved the ancient scheme of the Babylonian temple and palace hall, which was retained by the Assyrians in their palaces, but not in their temples; and if this be so, the monastic churches of the Tûr 'Abdîn are the last representatives of the oldest Oriental architecture. The walls and vault of the nave of Mâr Gabriel are devoid of ornament, but the vault of the central sanctuary is adorned with mosaics. The accumulated soot of centuries of candle-smoke has not entirely obscured the glory of its golden ground, of the great jewelled cross laid over the centre of the vault, and the twisted vine scrolls with which it is encircled. It is said that similar mosaics once covered the whole church and were destroyed by the soldiers of Tîmûr.

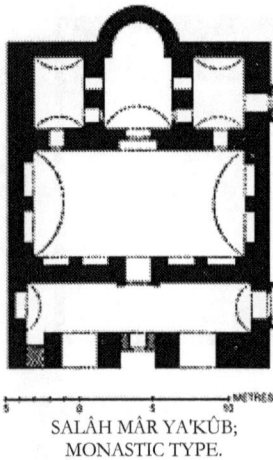

SALÂH MÂR YA'KÛB;
MONASTIC TYPE.

We rode next morning into Midyat and camped beside the ruined church of Mâr Philoxenos which, since it has not been recently repaired, is of greater interest than any other in the town. (Deir 'Umar, 5.30; Mezîzakh, 8.15; Midyâd, 9.15.)

I visited inside the town Mâr Shim'ûn, which is in process of being rebuilt, and Mâr Barsauma, which has been completely rebuilt. Outside the town is the monastery of Mâr Ibrahîm and Mâr Hôbel. It has recently been repaired, but much of the masonry is ancient. The two churches, dedicated to the two patron saints, belong to the monastic type of Mâr Gabriel; the mouldings round the doors, and the cyma cornice are old. There is also a small chapel, dedicated to the Virgin; it is square in plan and covered by a dome on squinches, but it appeared to me to be of later date. I was shown in this monastery a very remarkable silken vestment. The ground is of green satin covered with a repeated pattern in gold, silver and coloured silks, representing a woman in a red robe seated in a howdah upon the back of a camel. A man naked to the waist is seated upon the ground with his head bowed upon his hands. A variety of animals and floral motives are scattered round the principal figures. The subject is no doubt taken from the story of Leila and Majnûn. The date of this brocade is probably somewhere between 1560 and 1660. A fragment showing a like pattern is in the possession of Dr. Sarre. The monastery possesses besides a small bronze thurible, of which I succeeded in procuring a counterpart. A similar thurible exists in the British Museum (No. 540 in the catalogue of Early Christian and Byzantine Antiquities); it is said to have come from Mâr Musa el Habashi, between Damascus and Palmyra. The Kaiser Friedrich Museum has obtained several in Cairo and Trebizond (Wulff: *Altchristliche Bildwerke*, Teil I, nos. 967-970). These are ascribed to the sixth and seventh centuries. Mr. Dalton, to whom I owe this information, gives me references to two others, one in the Bargello collection at Florence (No. 241 in the catalogue of the Carraud Collection, published in 1898 and one published in the *Echos d'Orient*, VII., 1904, p. 148.)

The task of planning it was a labour of hatred. The population of Midyâd, men, women and children, stationed themselves upon the ruined walls, and for them it was no doubt the most entertaining afternoon which they had spent for many a long week, but for me, and for the patient bearers of the measuring tape, the hours were charged with exasperation. The Kâimmakâm, when he appeared upon this agitated scene (Midyâd is the seat of government in the Tûr 'Abdîn), succeeded in clearing the ruins for a few moments, but as soon as he had turned his back, the hordes reassembled with a greater zest than before.

My Christian servants returned in the evening from the bazaar gravely disquieted by the gossip which was current there. It was rumoured that the wave of massacre had spread to Aleppo and they trembled for the fate of their wives and families. The news which was causing us so much anxiety was in fact nearly a month old, but we did not learn until we reached Diyârbekr that Aleppo had escaped with a week of panic.

Diary Entries after Bell Left Mor Gabriel

21/05/1909

Friday May {22} 21. [21 May 1909] Left Der el Amer (Mor Gabriel Monastery) at 5.50, got to Mezizakh at 8.15 and to Der Mar Ibrahim a little after 9.

The monastery is built in fact[?] of the same very solid masonry as that of parts of Der el Amer. Flatly moulded caps outside and moulded jambs on the inner doors of Mar Hobel. I subsequently went back and planned it and saw the embroidered robe. Then planned Mar Philoxenos, a very interesting place.

The old church appears to have been of the arcaded type. An open narthex was subsequently added to the S and still later its doors were closed up and a porch added. Horrible crowds. The Kaimakam came to see me and was very civil. He says all is quiet, but Fattuh brings rumours of alarums and excursions.

22/05/1909

Sat. May {23} 22. [22 May 1909] Had an awfully long day beginning with 1/2 an hour's work on the basilica of Mar Philoxenos

which was I think a true basilica with the narthex to the W. Probably all vaulted; the old vault of the N aisle remains, of great stones, quite different from the new vaults. Rode off at 6.5 with Jusef and Abd ur Rahman and got to {Arnas} Salah

at {5.50} 7.25. The wonderful church lies to the W of the village. Stayed there till 9.20. It deserved a longer visit. Lots of mouldings, round the bottom of the narthex wall, round the inside of the nave (decorated and too high to take) doors etc. But horribly dark inside. Got to Arnas at 10.35 and stayed till 12.20.

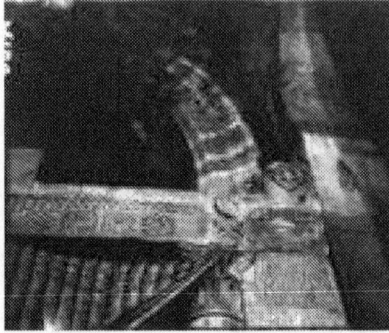

The church is much ruined - remains of the cymatium still to be seen outside. It has been restored but I think exactly on the old plan, ie the engaged piers here are part of the original structure. They fit onto the apse instead of leaving the awkward gap of the reconstruction piers. Lunched before I left. The church is part of a house (the buildings of Mar Yakub are also inhabited by peasants). Two {apses} niches on the E side of court, one apsed, but both much later work. We rode down hill and up to another village, Halaf, which we reached at 12.55. At 2 we got to Kefr Zeh

and stayed till 3.45. The church is inhabited by a nun
- there was also a Kas but I'm not sure if he lived there
- there was only one room. The piers here are part of a
reconstruction: I shd think the church was originally
vaulted from the walls only. Here and in both the
other chambers fine decorated mouldings round the
triumphal arch. I was very tired by the time I had
finished. We were told it was 3 hours to Khakh but it
was only a little over 2. We left Kefr Zeh at 3.45, {got
to} passed Mar Hanik at 4.50 and so onto a plateau

from which we presently saw Khakh lying on its hill with the mountains behind it - very beautiful. We had had thunderstorms all day and the evening was mild and lovely like an English spring. Got into camp at 5.50. After tea I took a look round and found that there was much to be done. Prayers were being said in the Adra, the women standing in the narthex, the men inside. One of the latter had put down his knife and half a cigarette in a holder on the narthex door step. As I came back through the village, the people coming up from prayers greeted me with "Marhaba Ingliziyeh." The Adra is occupied by a monk, a novice and a nun. The latter begged me to give them arms as a little time ago the Moslems came and said that order had been given that all Xians were to be killed. The Xians in Midyat heard the same thing and shut themselves into their houses for a day or two.

Summary of Salah, Arnas, and Kefarzeh Churches in Northern Tur Abdin

The next day was devoted to three churches which I visited and planned on the way to Khâkh, Mâr Yâ'kûb at Salâh, Mâr Kyriakos at Arnâs and Mâr 'Azîzîyeh at Kefr Zeh. I doubt whether there exists anywhere a group of buildings more precious to the archæologist than these three churches and the little domed shrine of the Virgin which stands almost perfect among the ruins of Khâkh (Fig. 201). It is close upon a miracle that in this forgotten region, long subjected to the tyranny of the Kurds, such masterpieces of architecture should have escaped destruction; the explanation is probably to be found in the rugged mountain frontiers of the Tûr 'Abdîn. Even though it lay upon the edge of country which was for over a hundred years the battle-ground of the Persian and the Byzantine, war seems to have penetrated but little into its heart. The Christian communities, from

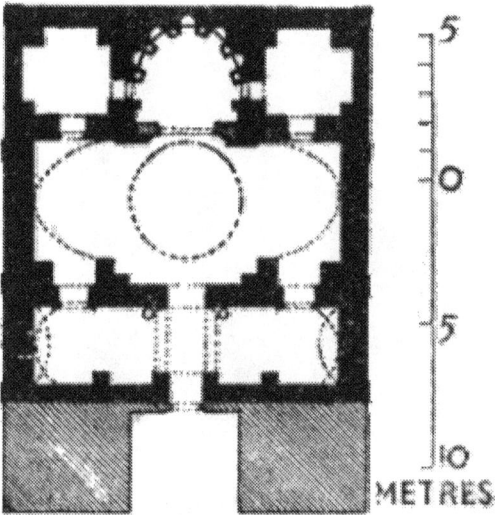

FIG. 201—KHA'KH, CHURCH OF
THE VIRGIN

their rock-cut cells in the crags of Mount Izala, must have listened to the rumours of advance and flight and siege; they could almost witness the encounter of armies in the plain below. But "the lofty mountain, precipitous and almost inaccessible," as Procopius describes it, was a sure refuge, and Procopius himself can scarcely have been acquainted with the wooded uplands and fertile valleys where already in his time stood the churches and monasteries of Salâh and Arnâs, Kefr Zeh and Khâkh. The Arab conquerors left the Christians undisturbed; they bowed the head and suffered under the fierce blast of Tîmûr's invasion and under the secular persecution of the Kurds; but decimated and stripped of their wealth, they held firmly to the bare walls of their religious houses, and the meagre, ragged choirs still chant their litanies under vaults which have withstood the assault of fourteen centuries. Into this country I came, entirely ignorant of its architectural wealth, because it was entirely unrecorded. None of the inscriptions collected by Pognon go back earlier than the ninth century; the plans which had

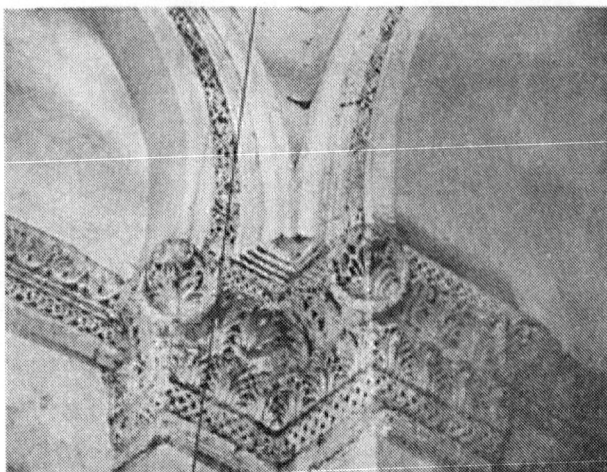

KHÂKH, CHURCH OF THE VIRGIN, CAPITALS.

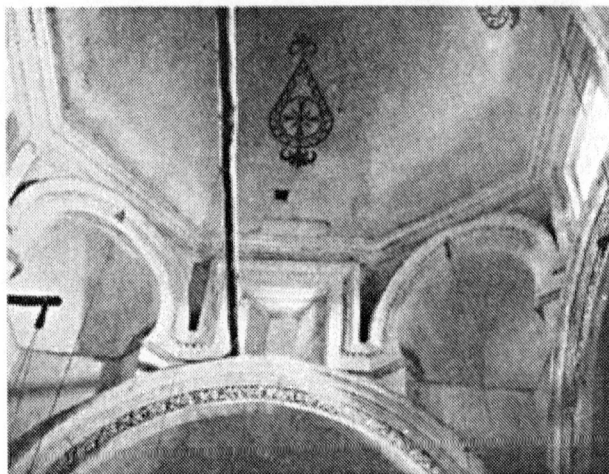

KHÂKH, CHURCH OF THE VIRGIN, DOME ON SQUINCH ARCHES.

THE CHELABÎ

FORDING THE TIGRIS BELOW DIYÂRBEKR.

been published were lamentably insufficient and were
unaccompanied by any photographs. When I entered Mâr
Yâ'kûb at Salâh and saw upon its walls mouldings and carved
string courses which bored the sign manual of the Græco-
Asiatic civilization I scarcely dared to trust to the conclusions
to which they pointed. But church after church confirmed
and strengthened them. The chancel arches, covered with an

exquisite lacework of ornament, the delicate grace of the acanthus capitals, hung with garlands and enriched with woven entrelac (Fig. 200), the repetition of ancient plans and the mastery of constructive problems which revealed an old architectural tradition, all these assure to the churches of the Tûr 'Abdîn the recognition of their honourable place in the history of the arts.

It was evening when we rode over the last of the wooded hills and saw the village of Khâkh lying upon a green knoll in the midst of a fertile plain. The rays of the setting sun touched the dome of the church of the Virgin, the tower of Mâr Sobo and the terraced houses; they flashed upon the pool below the village, by the edge of which my camp was pitched, and were mercifully unrevealing of poverty and ruin. It seemed to me that I had ended the most wonderful day since that which had brought me to Ukheidir by dropping into a village of the fifth century, complete and prosperous in every part. The searching light of morning disclosed a different picture. The houses were mere hovels, and except for the church of the Virgin not one of the ancient buildings but had fallen into the extremity of decay. That church is, however, the jewel of the Tûr 'Abdîn. It has suffered scarcely any change since the builders completed it, and it points a way to the solution of many a problem of Byzantine architecture. Its plan suggests a memorial rather than a monastic type; the domestic buildings near it are small and modern and I saw no trace of an ancient monastic house. A nun and the village priest occupied the rooms that now stand to the north of the courtyard. The nun was young and personable, and she found the religious life very much to her taste. Her sacred calling gave her the right to come and go as she pleased, to mix in male society and even to put forth her opinion in male councils. Moreover it provided her with an excuse for claiming audience of me on the evening of my arrival.

96

"I have come to see my sister," I heard her announce. "Does she speak Arabic?" And before Fattûh could answer, she had presented herself at the tent door. The object of her visit was to ask me for a revolver.

"What do you want with a revolver?" I said.

"We are afraid," she replied. "We are all afraid of massacre."

The little community of Jacobites snatch their daily bread from field and vineyard which lie at the mercy of marauding Kurds, whose practices were not, unfortunately, to remain for us a matter of hearsay. The second night at Khâkh was marked by the only misadventure that has befallen me in Turkey. We had intended to leave the village early on the following morning and everything was prepared for our departure; even my saddle-bags, duly packed with notebooks and camera, were lying ready in my tent. In the middle of the night I was awakened by a rustling noise, and starting up I saw the figure of a man crouched in the doorway. We had grown careless with months of safe journeying in dangerous places, and neither Fattûh nor I had taken the trouble to set a guard over the camp. The thieves had found us an easy prey; before the servants and zaptiehs were roused, they had made off into the night and we were left to reckon up our loss. What money I had with me had been taken out of my tent, the servants had been robbed of all their spare clothing and various other small objects were missing, but the real disaster was the disappearance of the saddle-bags which contained my note-books. We stood helpless, gazing into the darkness into which had vanished the results of four months' work. A rifle shot fired by Selîm had awakened the priest, who came hurrying down to inquire into our case. Deeply distressed was he, poor man, to hear of our misfortune, for we were the guests of the village, and he feared that ill might fall upon him and his flock for suffering us to come to harm. I listened to a great deal of divergent advice, and finally decided to send for the Chelabî, who is the feudal chief of the Kurdish tribes in the Tûr 'Abdîn. Accordingly at the first dawn Fattûh and a zaptieh were dispatched across the hills to bear him the news. A certain village lay under suspicion, a little robbers' nest situated in the depth of a wild and rocky valley a few miles to the east. The people of Khâkh were well used to the depredations of the men of Zâ'khurân, and during the course of the day we were provided with more positive evidence against them. It chanced that the thieves had carried off a parcel of my gloves, and these they shed along the path as they ran. Gloves lying upon the rocky ways of the Tûr 'Abdîn are exceptional objects, and the path by which they were found was that which led to Zâ'khurân. Evening brought the Chelabî, pacing sedately upon his mare with twenty men behind him, all dressed in white garments and armed with rifles. I went out to welcome them and brought their leader to my tents, where he listened to my tale over a cup of coffee and gave me many assurances of redress. This done, he repaired with great dignity to the roof of the priest's house, converted for the time into a court of justice, and received, until late into the night, deputations from the neighbouring villages. Next day the judgment seat was removed to Zâ'khurân, and Fattûh went with it as witness to the crime and representative of the plaintiff; at dusk he returned and reported that the Chelabî had arrested four men, selected, so far as could be ascertained, by empirical methods from among the inhabitants of the district, but that no clue had been found to the missing note-books. It was now time to invoke a higher power, and I entrusted a zaptieh with a letter to the Kâimmakâm of Midyâd and with a telegram which was to be sent from Midyâd to the Vâlî at Diyârbekr. The Kâimmakâm entered into the business like a man. On the following evening ten zaptiehs arrived from Midyâd, and next morning fifty foot soldiers marched into our camp. The nature of evidence is not clearly grasped in the East, and by the third day after the robbery there was no person in the country-side, except, I believe, myself, against whom a charge of complicity had not been raised, but there continued to be no further proof than that which we had had from the beginning, and it pointed to Zâ'khurân. To Zâ'khurân, therefore, the miniature army took its way, leaving me divided between regret for the disturbance which my own carelessness had brought about, and gratitude for the good-will displayed on every side. So difficult, however, had it become to protect the innocent, that but for the notebooks I should have left the guilty in peace. My servants were plunged in grief; their honour was gone—indeed whose honour was left intact?—and in sackcloth and ashes we passed the day. And then . . . in the grey dawn we were wakened by a voice shouting from the hills: "Your goods are here! your goods are here!" Every man in the camp leapt up and ran in the direction of the sound, and there, lying upon a rock among the oak scrub, was all that we had lost. Nothing had been injured, nothing was missing, except some money, which was subsequently refunded to me by the Ottoman government, at the instance of the British Vice-Consul in Diyârbekr—and it may well be questioned whether any other government would have recognized a like liability. The villagers of Khâkh assembled round the tents and shed tears of thankfulness over the recovered objects, and I mounted in haste and rode off to Zâ'khurân to set a term to the pursuit of criminals. The cause of the restitution was there apparent. The village was deserted; men, women and children had fled into the hills taking with them all that they possessed, and it was reported by a picket that the Chelabî and the soldiers were engaged in capturing the flocks of the community. I sent a messenger after them and rode myself to Midyâd to ask for a universal amnesty. Revenge is not so sweet as it is said to be, nor is it so easy when wrong is afoot to determine who is the more wronged.

23/05/1909

Sun. May {24} 23. [23 May 1909] - I see I've got the days wrong somewhere and am a day on; now it's right. Thunder and heavy rain when I woke. Worked all day at the 2 churches here, the Adra and Mar Saba. The Adra is perfect but for the dome outside which was rebuilt 2 years ago by the Xians - to the great distress of the monk. Since the rebuilding the water comes in which it never did before. He says the old roof was incredibly solid. I don't think the church can be later than the 5th c. Splendid decorated mouldings. The [sketch] acanthus everywhere, with entrelacs, bead and reel, and vine rinceaux round the door from the narthex to the church. Mar Saba has been restored. The piers are later both in nave and aisles. I think the church was a basilica, but with solid walls broken only by doors between the nave and aisles. The difficulty is that the doors are all moulded on the aisle side, which seems very odd, especially in the N aisle where there is no entrance but from the church. Was the whole N aisle a later addition and the church only a nave with a narthex on the S side? Yes, the whole aisle is new - straight ..... in E wall. The N doors would then be outer doors. There is the usual apse to the E of the S court - this time I think original. N of Mar Saba another little church too full of fleas to work at. Elaborately decorated door bet. narthex and nave but later work than the other 2. Its small late chapel further W. Outside the town to the N is Mar [space left blank] - late, one monk inhabits it. To the E Miriam Aghuthaitha with a tower, late, a dome on squinches, and Mar Johanna of the same date I shd say as the church N of Mar Saba - a decorated door which I photographed.

Theft in Tur Abdin

24/05/1909

Monday May 24. [24 May 1909] In the night we were robbed. I woke and found a man in my tent, gave the alarm, but they were off having dévalizéd us. At the first dawn sent Fattuh and Abd ur Rahman to Mezezakh to fetch the Chelabi ibn Ismail who owns this country from Jezireh [Cizre] to Mardin. At once they found a bag of change on the path leading to Zakhuran and later in the day a shepherd brought in one of my gloves found further along the road. At 5 the Chelabi arrived with a large and picturesque following robed in white and armed with rifles. After visiting me he held a mejlis in the der. Before sunset 14 men came in from Zakhuran, all swearing they knew nothing of the matter. Read the Bible in Spain - splendid book.

25/05/1909

Tuesday May 25. [25 May 1909] The Chelabi visited me in the morning and I told him I wd ruin the world if my things did not appear. All the govts of Europe said the priest wd present themselves in force. The good Chelabi then rode off to Zakhuran with Fattuh and all his party- and I went to Der es Salib. It belongs to the later period. The church down a long dark passage, narthex, nave crossways and 3 sanctuary chambers. No decoration inside but a late decorated apse in the court with the usual cross in its roof. At the SW corner of the outer wall some very big stones but I doubt whether any part belongs to the older period. It is 21/4 hours from here. We passed a late ruined monastery and village on our way. At 6 Fattuh came back. The Chelabi picked up another glove on the road. He is calling in all the Mukhtars and is to bring the suspects here tomorrow. I sent one of my soldiers to Midyat with a letter to the Kaimakam asking for soldiers tomorrow at dawn. Things look brighter - Informers are beginning to turn up. Two villages are suspect and it is clear that there are plenty of people who know where the things are.

26/05/1909

Wed May 26. [26 May 1909] The Chelabi came back in the morning with 5 prisoners selected I fancy at haphazard, but no news of my goods. I finished The Bible in Spain. In the evening 10 zaptiehs arrived. During the day some men of Zakhuran proposed to search the hills and bring the things next morning.

27/05/1909

Thurs. May 27. [27 May 1909] But nothing arrived. The Chelabi went off to Zakhuran with the Zaptiehs after taking an affectionate farewell of me. I rode out that way to see a ruined church but found nothing interesting. While I was away 50 infantry with 3 officers arrived. They were Mulazim Muhammad Agha, Zaptieh Ibrahim Chowwish (who spoke a little French) and Askari Mulazim Suleiman Effendi, the old man who came to see me while I was at Midyat. The priest tells me that the exedras in the courts of the monasteries are where the bp said the week day prayers, the church being used only on Sunday. The inscrips in the exedra here (there are a good many) are all tombstones of monks, without dates, he says. They were simply written on the interior of the exedra at any time. I then went to the Adra and re-measured it, the officers taking a friendly interest. They were most kind. After lunch came a message from the Chelabi that man woman and child had fled from Zakhuran, taking the flocks with them. The soldiers therefore prepared to depart - they were sitting in a temporary shelter on the monastery roof. The Mulazim gave each man a very coarse loaf, they formed up, blew their trumpet and marched away, taking with them the 5 prisoners and the Mukhtar of Khakh, Melkeh. I felt dreadfully concerned at all this. Everyone now is under suspicion including the Chelabi, and a whole village has been driven into the hills. I remeasured the ruined church. We decided in the evening that I shd go with the caravan to Diarbekr [Diyarbakir (Amida)] and leave Fattuh with the Chelabi.

28/05/1909

Friday May 28. [28 May 1909] But in the grey dawn one of the villagers woke us shouting from the ruined tombs on the opposite hill that our things were there. It appeared that a man from Zakhuran had told him. My servants rushed off and found everything except the money, Fattuh's clothes, a camera strap and 3 anticas. So we breakfasted and I sent the camp on to Midyat while I rode off with Fattuh, Abd ul Ghani Effendi (he arrived last night - I don't know what his duties are) and 2 zaptiehs to Zakhuran which we reached in 11/2 hours. It was completely deserted except for cocks and hens; the Chelabi and the soldiers had gone into the hills to fetch the flocks. It lay in a deep rocky valley, a regular robbers' nest. I lay down under a ruin on the top of the hill and went to sleep while the others sat under an oak tree. When I woke a bp from Karboran had joined the party - dressed in purple with a gold and jewelled cross, Urfa [Sanliurfa (Edessa)] work. So it being near 11 I lunched and talked to the bp who said he had seen me in Jerusalem [(El Quds esh Sherif, Yerushalayim)]. He spoke well of the Chelabi - said he was a friend to the Xians which I believe from the care he took of Khakh. The sheep were seen coming in but still no Chelabi. I wrote various notes at the request of the bp for the release of Melkeh and the return of Xian sheep which had been swept in with the rest. This was under a tree by the village - a few red eyed women had returned by this time. At about 12 I rode off with Fattuh, Abd el Rahim and a Zakhuran man. We went by extraordinarily rocky barren valleys, the villages on the hill tops like little forts. We passed near Kefr Zeh and Arnas and got into camp at 6. The Kaimmakam and others visited me and after sunset I went and looked again at the ruined church.

Letter to Mother about the Robbery

Friday May 28. [28 May 1909]

Friday May 28. [28 May 1909] Oh my dear Mother we've had such a week! Now that we have come to the end of our terrible adventure, and to a prosperous end, I must tell you about it, but while it was going on I could think of nothing else. Well, we left Midyat on Saturday and I had a long day, seeing and planning on my way to Khakh 3 wonderful churches. I got in to Khakh late in the afternoon and found my camp pitched by a great pool below a charming village and at my very tent door one of the most remarkable churches I have ever seen, 5th century if not 4th, domed, with exquisite carved mouldings - in short perfect, and all standing. There was another ruined church higher up the village and various other buildings that needed examination; I took a hasty survey of them before sunset and determined that things of this kind could not be dismissed in a hurry and I must spend the next day at Khakh. This resolve was warmly applauded by the priest and the nun who inhabited the church and I accordingly passed the whole day planning, photographing and incidentally solving one or two difficult points that have puzzled me for the past 2 years. For the buildings in this country are a revelation and their importance has certainly not yet been recognized. So I went to bed well pleased after having prepared everything for an early start next day, packed my 2 notebooks (which were now almost full of plans) into my saddle bags, together with my camera and everything needed for the day's work, and put my riding clothes ready on the chair by my bed. In the middle of the dark night a rustling woke me; I looked up and saw a man crouching in my tent, a shadowy figure outlined against the sky. I tore open the mosquito curtain, lept [sic] out of bed and made for him, but while I got myself out of the mosquito net he had had time to get himself out of my tent and I just saw him disappear between the tents, I shouted to my servants who had chosen that night to sleep like the dead and it must have been a full minute before I roused them. Of course one of the two soldiers with me ought to have been on guard, especially as neither of them had done anything but sleep all day while I was working - but they only slept all the sounder by night. Finally we were all roused (and I remembered that I was standing chatting in my nightgown so I retired to put on a skirt but first I looked round to see if anything was missing. Everything lying loose was gone, clothes, saddle bags, boots and half one of my mule trunks had been emptied and the contents (including a belt with œT42 in it) taken away. Far the greatest misfortune, however, was that the two notebooks in my saddle bags contained every scrap of work that I had done since the beginning of the journey, except the big ground plan of Khethar [Ukhaydir]. And to crown all, Jusef came with the news that the bag containing every finished film since Baghdad was gone too. So in a moment there was a clean sweep, photographs, plans, notes, all had vanished - Rakka [Ar Raqqah], Samarra, half Khethar, all the churches at which I had toiled, all the odds and ends along the road: I might just as well not have travelled at all. I was overwhelmed. There we stood helpless in the dark night while my goods were hurrying away somewhere over the rocky hills and through the oak woods. At this point arrived the priest, who had been roused by two shots that my servants had fired into the night, and everyone began to give me his advice. I had an hour or two before the dawn came to consider what was best to be done and I decided to send Fattuh and a soldier to fetch the Chelabi who lived in a village about 7 hours away. Now the Chelabi is the great magnate of the district. All the people, from Jezireh [Cizre] to Mardin, all the Tur Abdin, belong to him; they are his tribe and he rules them with far more authority than the government possesses. Moreover, if I sent for soldiers they would be quartered on the villagers of Khakh, who were, I was pretty sure, guiltless. Anyhow I determined to send for the Chelabi first. We had a clue. In the afternmoon three men from Zakhuran, a village about 2 hours away with a very bad reputation, had been seen hanging about the

106

tents; when dawn broke, we found a little bag containing loose change lying on the path to Zakhuran and later in the day, a shepherd brought in a glove that he had found about an hour away on the same path. Meantime Fattuh had gone and I had nothing to do but to wait for the Chelabi. I spent the whole day reading the Bible in Spain, which Mrs Ramsay had given me, and that magical book carried me far away from all my troubles and took me wandering up and down the rocky hills of Spain without a thought for anyone but Borrow. (Will you please give me a complete edition of him for my birthday? He is, without doubt, one of the greatest of writers and I one of the most illiterate of people.) In the evening arrived the Chelabi, pacing on his mare through the stony paths with 20 armed men behind him and Fattuh by his side. In great state the Chelabi was brought to my tent, a splendid handsome Kurd he is, the six feet of him robed in white and cloaked in a gold embroidered abbayah. So we sat and drank coffee while he heard my tale (he hasn't much Arabic, but the priest interpreted in Kurdish) and finally the Chelabi and his men walked away in procession and took up their abode on the roof of the priest's house. No sooner had he arrived than deputations from all the villages came pouring in - the Chelabi had sent word to each of them - and he held his court on the monastery roof. So the evening passed, but no decision was reached. Next day the Chelabi and Fattuh and all the party rode off to Zakhuran to make an inquest there. I spent the time examining some churches among the hills and in the evening Fattuh came back and said that matters had not advanced. I was in despair. The more I thought of all my vanished work, the more miserable I became. That night I sent a soldier in to Midyat with a letter to the Kaimmakam asking for soldiers, and also telegrams to the Vali and the consul at Diarbekr [Diyarbakir (Amida)]. The Chelabi came back the following morning with 5 prisoners, selected, I fancy, pretty much at haphazard - oh, I must tell you, they found another glove upon the Zakhuran road, which was providential, a glove in the Tur Abdin being a most incriminating piece of evidence. At night 10 zaptiehs arrived from Midyat and early the next day a body of 50 infantry with 3 officers. The Kaimmakam had entered into the business like a man. At dawn the Chelabi and the zaptiehs all went off to Zakhuran to renew the process of intimidation. I found it almost impossible to preserve a sober judgment. No one knew anything and everybody accused everybody else. At the same time it was quite certain that a great many people must be in the secret and rightly or wrongly I suspected the head man of Khakh of having information. But I began to make my deuil of my notebooks and with a heavy heart measured and photographed the Khakh churches all over again. Something at any rate had to be saved from the wreck. The 3 officers were kindness itself, indeed I can't say enough in their praise. The Chelabi worked like a Trojan, but he had a personal reason, poor dear, for in the end suspicion was bound to rest on him as the head of the tribe, as in fact it does now rest, though I am persuaded unjustly and I mean to clear him before the government at Diarbekr. In the afternoon he sent back word that man, woman and child had fled from Zakhuran, carrying with them all the sheep and cattle into the hills. At this, the officers got ready, called up their men from the monastery roof, gave them their rations, and taking with them the 5 prisoners and the headman of Khakh, marched away to Zakhuran. I have seldom spent a more unhappy evening. I bitterly regretted my carelessness in not having seen myself that a watch was being kept; if the master forgets, the men are bound to forget too. The truth was we had all grown thoughtless with so much safe travelling through dangerous places, and we needed a lesson. But it was a bitter one. I had brought confusion everywhere and driven a whole village into the hills; if it had not been for all the hard work that had disappeared with my notebooks, I should have recalled the soldiers, let the thing go and paid the price, but as it was, the price was too big and besides I had gone too far. Fattuh was just as unhappy and we were both on the point of swearing that we would never travel again. I decided that evening that I would leave him with the Chelabi and myself go away to Diarbekr. I was only giving more trouble and I was doing no good, whereas if I left Fattuh, he would be of use to the Chelabi and if the things were found he could bring them to me. So it was settled. And then what do you think happened? In the grey dawn we were wakened by a man of the village shouting to us "Your goods have come back! your goods have come back!" All the servants set off running up the rocky hill, opposite the camp and there on a big stone they found everything, piled in a heap. Everything but the money which was after all the least important. So peace was restored and all the village came to congratulate us and I sent the camp into Midyat and went off with Fattuh to Zakhuran, to save the honour of the Chelabi. But when we got to Zakhuran - we were joined by several officials, I must tell you, and some stray zaptiehs, a strange party - we found the village absolutely deserted. Every soul had fled and the Chelabi and the soldiers had gone off into the hills to sieze the cattle. We sent word to them and decided to wait a few hours - it was still only 8 o'clock. I went to sleep and the others sat under an oak tree and smoked cigarettes. When I woke I was not at all surprised to find that a bishop had joined the party. There he sat in his purple robes with a gold and jewelled cross in his hands and we entered into amicable conversation while I eat my lunch under the oak tree. He had come, good man, to protect his diocese, for incidentally, it appeared that the Chelabi had swept up sheep belonging to two Christian villages in the hills - Zakhuran is Moslem and such a robbers' nest as it looked lying in its deep stony valley, I never hope to see again. By this time it was noon and I had 6 hours' ride in to Midyat, so I wrote various letters to the Chelabi and the officers, asking for the return of the Christian sheep and the release of the headman of Khakh (this rather reluctantly) and then we took our leave of the bishop and the rest and made our way back to Midyat. There I found the Kaimmakam and the officials all at my beck and call, having received peremptory telegrams from Diarbekr where the consul had not been idle. I sent telegrams and received another bishop and gave instructions to the Kaimmakam, and having borrowed œT5 from him, this morning (Sat. May 29 [29 May 1909]) I left for Diarbekr. On the way I met a dragoman whom the consul had sent post haste to my aid, a worthy Armenian who is rather a bore, for he has turned back with me and I am obliged to entertain him, honest[?] man. I think I shall get all the money back, for the Chelabi will produce it and eventually I don't doubt that he will lay his hands on the thief or thieves, but I'm heartily ashamed of the whole business and would cheerfully give a great deal more than I lost to blot it out. However, there it is, and Fattuh and I will know better in future, Inshallah. I haven't much pity for the villagers of Zakhuran for when they are not robbing me they are pillaging the Christian villages and these last can get no redress. But as far as I know we are no nearer to finding the real offenders, though Heaven alone can tell how many prisoners the Chelabi has taken by this time! The methods of Turkish justice are simple, but they are very effective and as Sir Alfred says, it does more good to punish the wrong man than the right one for it frightens everybody into good behaviour. Still though I agree with this in principle I would rather not have it put into practice on my behalf.

Journey to Ancient Amida (Diyarbakir)

29/05/1909

Sat May 29. [29 May 1909] At which I did a few minutes work in the morning. Then with Fattuh to the shop of one Galleh Hormuz, a rich merchant. He took me to Mar Shimuneh where I saw two evangils, one illuminated. Then back to the shop to interview the other bp about the Xian sheep. He abused the Chelabi and so did Galleh; they said Zakhuran was his own people, the Mukhtar his cousin, he wd certainly try to get them off at the expense of the Xians. So I wrote a letter for the release of the sheep of Shahrika and Shapisna and gave it to the Kaimmakam who had now turned up. I borrowed £T5 off him and set off at 7.55 with a very nice zaptieh. At 8.30 we passed Este. At 10.15 we got to Kenderib[?] and found there Thomas Effendi, the dragoman from Diarbekr [Diyarbakir (Amida)] with 3 esterlis. So I dismissed my zaptieh with regret and at 10.50 we rode off together. He gave me news of the massacres at Adana [(Seyhan, Ataniya)] and said they had all been in fear of their lives. At 11.20 we reached Apsheh. At 12.15 we lunched under a tree for 1/2 an hour - poor Thomas

111

had come 16 hours yesterday - 5 today before he met me. At 1.10 Haldakh. Then into rocky hills and down a valley to Killeth which we reached at 4. Thomas knows the Yezidis well. He says Malek Ta'ous is the fallen angel and the Yezidis worship him because they think God will some day take him back into favour and then it will be best to be on the right side of Him. They are all Kurds.

30/05/1909

Sunday May 30. [30 May 1909] Off at 5.45 and by a beautiful valley full of vinyards [sic], water loving poplars by the stream, to Ahmedeh, 7.5. We saw Saun[?] in the hills. Then down the valley, narrow here, past a ruined church and up a hill to the W onto an upland. We saw at 10.30 Gireki Hajji Faris to the right about a mile away. At 11.20 Girreh Azair. 12.15 to 12.50 lunch at Isa Punar. At 1.20 Koghiyyeh by a tell. At 2.10 the Sheikhan Chai with Kara Punar on the other side. Uplands all covered with corn. Till the fall of Abdul Hamid this road was too dangerous to take, on account of the robbers. At 3.35 Hajjiyyet Turkan (Turkman, Kizil Bash) and at 4.45 Kerkha (Kurd) lying under its big mound. A long day.

31/05/1909

Monday May 31. [31 May 1909] We left Kerkha at 5.45 and forded the Tigris at 6.35. At 7.5 we came to Holan, at 8.45 to Satli Keui - all this across flattish country all cultivated. At 10.5 we passed Sadi Keui on the right. We had already sighted the minarets of Diarbekr [Diyarbakir (Amida)] far away, now they were quite close, and the great walls standing up on the high Tigris bank. We forded the river again - it was rather deep and came into mulberry gardens, through which we rode and up a paved road into the Mardin gate at 11. I went straight to the Consulate and found that Mr E Rawlins had gone to meet me by another road. She greeted me most kindly (she was a Miss Kappus the niece of Lütticke) and insisted on my staying with them though her baby is not 4 weeks old. I found 2 month's post waiting for me and while I was reading letters, Mr R. came in. In the evening appeared Miss Baldwin who is a nurse come out to help Dr and Mrs Ward (Americans) to found a hospital, a nice woman. Diarbekr is much disturbed. A massacre was only avoided by a miracle. The local committee intercepted a telegram from C'ple [Istanbul (Constantinople)] to the Ferik on Ap 17 ordering disturbances. A member of the committee showed a copy 3 weeks later to Thomas Effendi. For a few hours the town was in a panic. Mr R. walked through the streets quieting the people. The Ashraf are very anti Xian and anti Constitution. They have looted Ibrahim Pasha; all the Kurdish tribes turned against him as soon as he fell. The very men who are appointed to judge the case of Abd ul Hamid and his 2 brothers are at present riding on the former's best mares which they have taken. Yet the Committee from C'ple appointed after the fall of I. Pasha found the sons guiltless and so reported. I. Pasha was a great protector of the Xians and had many prosperous Xian villages many of which are now looted. Went to see the acting Vali who was the man who instigated the massacres in the Kizil Bash country - Devsim - the other day.

Summary of Trip to Diyarbakir

113

Two days and a half of journeying brought us to Diyârbekr. The way was without interest, except for that which was supplied by the dragoman of the British Consulate, who had

DIYÂRBEKR, MARDÎN GATE.

DIYÂRBEKR, YENI KAPU.

DIYÂRBEKR, CHEMIN DE RONDE, NORTH WALL.

DIYÂRBEKR, COURT OF ULU JÂMI'.

come to Midyâd to help me out of difficulties. A cheerful travelling companion he proved, and a well-informed. We camped on the second evening under the mound of Karkh, not far from the Tigris, and shortened our way next day by fording the river, which was now a shallow stream, and cutting across a wide bend. This route had the advantage of giving us a first view of Diyârbekr under its finest aspect. It stands upon the high crest of the Tigris bank, a great fenced city built of basalt—"black are the dogs and black the walls and black the hearts of black Amid," says the proverb. Since the days when Ammianus Marcellinus took part in the desperate resistance to Sapor, and watched from the towers of Amida the Persian hosts "collected for the conflagration of the Roman world," the din of battle has never been far from Diyârbekr. The town passed to and fro between the Byzantine and the Sassanian. Constantius fortified it and lost it to Sapor; Anastasius recaptured it and lost it to Kobâd and won it back; Justinian rebuilt the fortifications, but it fell with Mesopotamia to the Moslem invaders. The Kurdish Marwânds made it their capital, and after them the Turkmân Ortukids; Tîmûr burst through the famous walls and put the inhabitants to the sword, and finally the Turk conquered it in A.D. 1515 and holds it still. But there is no peace for the lawless capital of Kurdistân. Warring faiths struggle together as fiercely as rival empires, and the conflict is embittered by race hatreds. The heavy air, lying stagnant between the high walls, is charged with memories of the massacres of 1895, and when I was in Diyârbekr the news from Cilicia had rekindled animosity and fear. Moslem and Christian were equally persuaded that the other was watching for an opportunity to spring at his throat. Tales of fresh outbreaks in different parts of the empire were constantly circulated in the bazaars, and the men who listened went home and fingered at their rifles. If there had been any sign of further disturbance at Constantinople, Diyârbekr would have run with blood.

With the population in this temper it would have been futile to inquire into the prospects of constitutional government. I spent a day among ancient churches. I have published photographs and plans of the Jacobite church of the Virgin and the Greek Orthodox church of Mâr Cosmo in *Amida*: Van Berchem and Strzygowski.

I spent a day upon the walls, which are as fine an example of mediæval fortification as any that exists. They hang, upon the south and south-east sides, high over the Tigris—it was from this direction that Sapor's troops effected an entry through a hollow passage that led down to the water's edge. On the south-west they crown a slope set thick with gardens of mulberry and vine, and towards the north the wall bends round to join the curve of the river. Four great gateways break this circuit. The Mardîn Gate commands the terraced gardens, and the road that passes through it runs down to an ancient bridge over the Tigris (Fig. 206). To the north-west and north the Aleppo or Mountain Gate and the Kharpût Gate open on to a fertile plain, and the Yeni Kapu, the New Gate, stands above the precipitous southern bank.

The Yeni Kapu differs in plan from the other three. It has square bastions, whereas they are protected on either side by massive round towers. The round towers extend all along the northern parts of the wall; on the other sides the towers are rectangular.

The lie of the ground makes it certain that the oldest fortifications of the city must have occupied much the same position as those which still surround it, and though the latter are proved by numerous inscriptions to be Mohammadan work of different periods, I should judge them to be built mainly upon ancient foundations. The north wall with its round towers is perfectly preserved; even the domed chambers inside the towers, together with the stairs that gave access to the *chemin de ronde*, are intact. All the arches and domes in the interior of the towers are of brick. Between the Kharpût and the Aleppo Gates a small aqueduct brings water to the town, the few springs within the walls being unpleasantly brackish. The citadel commands the north-east angle above the river; most of the space surrounded by its enclosing wall is occupied by modern buildings and by a mound whereon stood the castle of the first Mohammadan princes. The domed arsenal is said to have been a Christian church, but remembering my unsuccessful attempts to visit the arsenal at Baghdâd, I did not ask permission to enter it.

From a postern gate in the north wall a road leads down to the river, passing under a cliff out of which gushes a sulphurous spring. As I watched the soldiers of the garrison washing their clothes in its waters, I tried to reconcile it with "the rich spring, drinkable, indeed, but often tainted with hot vapours," which Ammianus Marcellinus describes as rising under the citadel, and to see the men of the 5th Parthian Legion in the ragged groups standing about it. His phrase "under the citadel but in the very heart of Amida" is difficult to understand. It does not seem to imply a spring outside the walls, yet there is no place "under the citadel" and within the walls.

From the citadel we walked to the Mardîn Gate along the *chemin de ronde*, a fine course, lifted high above the close air of the city and swept by the breezes that come down from Taurus (Fig. 208). Between the Aleppo Gate and the Mardîn Gate stand two huge round towers, larger than any others and later in date. One is known by inscriptions to have been erected by the Ortokid Sultan Malek Shah in the year A.D. 1208-1209, and the other must belong to the same period. The inscriptions have been published by Van Berchem, see Lehmann-Haupt: *Materialen zur älteren Geschichte Armeniens und Mesopotamiens*, p. 140. They are more fully published in *Amida*, but that work has not appeared in time for me to make any accurate reference to it.

Near the Mardîn Gate the *chemin de ronde* is for some distance vaulted over and lighted only by small loop-hole windows on the inner side. To the south of the Mardîn Gate the wall runs out abruptly, and the salient angle thus formed holds a great hall of which the vault is borne on columns. The two main streets lie from gate to gate, intersecting each other at right angles, and since this is in accordance with an ancient scheme of city planning, the line of the streets may be as old as the first foundation of the town. Not far from the point of intersection stands the Ulu Jami' with its famous courtyard, enclosed to east and west by a two-storeyed portico, which has been conjectured to be either the remains of a church built by Heraclius or a Byzantine palace (Fig. 209). The buildings need a more exhaustive / *p.326* / study than the fanaticism of the Mohammadan population will at present admit, and the correct plan of mosque and court has yet to be made. The older part of the work is closely related to the ancient architecture of the Tûr 'Abdîn.

Even this hasty survey of Diyârbekr was sufficient to convince me that the treasures which it contains are still unexplored. Of its many mosques only the Ulu Jami' has been so much as photographed, though the square minarets scattered over the town are probably an indication of an early date. Once or twice as I walked in the bazaars I looked through gateways into the courts of splendid khâns, where the walls were decorated with contrasted patterns in limestone and basalt, and stripes of black and white masonry are used in many of the houses and mosques. The final history of Amida must wait upon a much more careful investigation of the town than any which has yet been undertaken. (from Amuath to Amurath, Bell, 1924)

Letter to Home

Monday May 31 [31 May 1909]

Monday May 31 [31 May 1909] Diarbekr [Diyarbakir (Amida)]. I arrived here this morning after a prosperous journey with the good old dragoman - his name is Thomas Effendi. And here I am staying with the consul and his wife, Rawlins is their name, she is a German and he nephew of the Eton master. She had a baby 3 weeks ago, poor dear, and I feel I ought not to be bothering them but they insisted on my coming. And here I found an immense mail - all the delayed letters from Baghdad and letters from you and Father here. I think nothing has missed and I must tell you how rejoiced I was to have them. Also a letter from Elsa and one from Moll telling about the death of the poor little Paul - I am so very sorry about it and sympathise deeply. I telegraphed to you as soon as I arrived and I hope perhaps you will telegraph to me here. You are busy with the army! it's splendid of you. I feel an awful beast for not being there to take a hand too. Tell Father his long long letter about his journey was perfectly delightful and I read the tale of the adventures of the lady with the utmost excitement - but I think I agree with Mother in not wishing to admit her as yet to the recesses of the innocent family circle. I had a delightful letter from Hanagan too which I must answer. I have some work to do here so I expect I shall be kept 4 or 5 days. Things are quiet now but it was touch and go. There can be no doubt that Abd ul Hamid ordered a massacre of all Christians and why it only took place at Adana [(Seyhan, Ataniya)], I can't think. However, Heaven be praised! The country I am now going through is perfectly peaceful.

Ever your affectionate daughter

Gertrude.

Diary Entries about Diyarbakir

01/06/1909

Tuesday June 1. [1 June 1909] Wrote letters most of the day. The Wards and Miss Baldwin came to tea after which Mr R. [Rawlins] and I rode down to the bridge. It is supposed to be Roman but I did not see anything earlier than what might have been Arabic. The arches on the E side (or on the S side, left bank) are different from the others, the bridge here considerably narrower and on the lower side the arches are of alternate black and white stones. The old khans in Diarbekr [Diyarbakir (Amida)]

are built in the same way. There is one inside the Mardin gate and another in the bazaar where my caravan put up. Also many of the mosques are striped and the modern houses inside the courts are adorned with patterns and stripes of white. Half the bazaar was burnt down in 1895 at the time of the massacres. It is very attractive, shaded with trees, but dirty!

02/06/1909

Wed June 2 [2 June 1909] Went out early and planned 2 churches, the Jacobite and the Chaldaean. The former was particularly interesting, both originally of the same period. In the afternoon worked as well as I could at the mosque. The N,E and W sides of the old palace court remain. Byz. of the period of all the churches I have been seeing, ie 4th - 6th - probably nearer the former. We had a violent thunderstorm and rain after which Mr R [Rawlins] and I walked out round the walls and saw the inscriptions {(cufic)} and ...... on the 4 bastions between the Mardin and Aleppo Gates.

03/06/1909

Thurs June 3. [3 June 1909] Walked round the top of the walls with Thomas Effendi from the Kharput Gate to the Mardin Gate then down and into the great chamber S of that gate and then outside as far as the Yeni Kapu. The other 3 gates are all of the Edessa-Cairo pattern, with 2 big round bastions and a quite simple moulded doorway. In the Aleppo gate there were 2 doors[?] - perhaps 3. There are also a few posterns. The 2 main streets cross the city from the 4 gates. The oldest part of the walls is from the Aleppo gate to the river where all the bastions are round. The great inscribed bastions are certainly later - they have stalactite work on the top - and from this point most of the towers are square. The interior arches and domes and vaults are everywhere of brick. Fine shallow domes in the chambers in the old round bastions. The Yeni Kapu over the river is quite a different pattern, with one square bastion on the E side. After I had come in Mrs Thomas came to see me and also Hajji 'Adleh, I. Pasha's second wife, a fine determined looking woman. She came to ask my help for the sons and brought with her a bright eyed Xian servant, the only one of their servants who had not deserted them. Khansa Khatun, the chief wife is with the tribe. She is reported to be a very able woman. The Milleh are nearly blotted out. After lunch walked down to the citadel, photographed the arch of the Serai with its curious relief and inscrip. (I do not think the latter is Arabic) and took photographs from the top of the mound. All the work of the citadel seems to belong to the Arab period. Went to see Mrs Thomas and to tea with the Wards.

04/06/1909

Friday June 4. [4 June 1909] Off at 7. Thomas Effendi rode with me to the barracks outside the town. There is a kiosk on a hill a little way off which is said to have been built for Sultan Murad when he came fighting here. At 8 we passed Shilbe, at 9.5 Uch Keui - all the country flat. At 10.45 we crossed the deep valley of the Dere Gechid Chai; at 11 the tiny village of Tolek on the top of the further side of the valley and so out onto the plain again. Mostly cultivated but the crops not good. From 12 to 12.35 lunched. At 1 we crossed the little Kara Khan Chai and at 2.45 got to Tarmul where there is a village on a mound and a small khan. Cool delicious weather [....]

124

Photos of the First Visit to Tur Abdin

Embedded column at Mor Augen monastery which today is not occupied and under Turkish military control.

Mor Augen

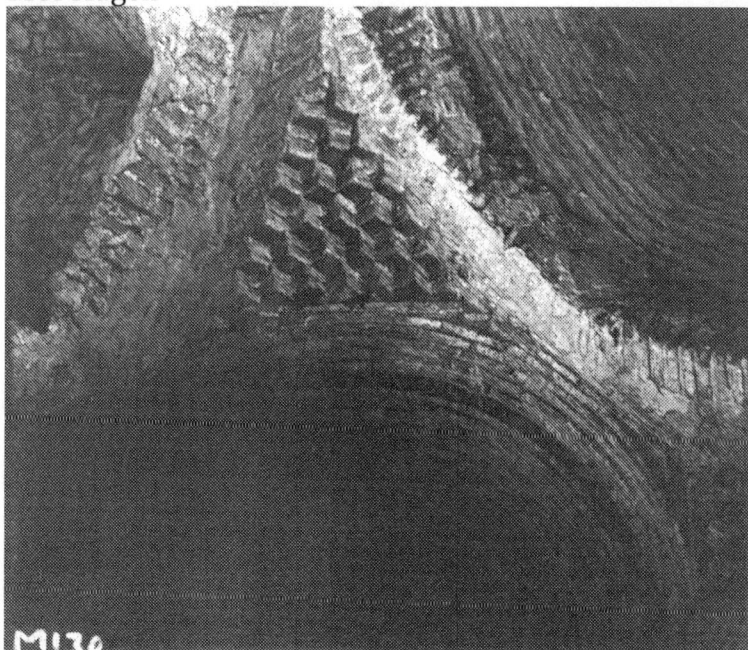

Unique brick work in the asp of Mor Augen

Mor Augen doorway. This is typical of many of the church doors in the region. It is small and low mainly for security reasons.

Mt. Izla and Mor Augen monastery

Mor Augin courtyard

Views of courtyard of Mor Augen

Cell of Mor Augen

Mor Gabriel Monastery courtyard outside church
entrance

View from Mor Gabriel

View from Mor Gabriel

A view approaching Mor Gabriel

Tomb of the Egyptians at Mor Gabriel

Arnas Church interior

Diyabakir church (Amida)

Kefarzeh Church exterior

Church of Khah as Bell called it. Today it is known as Hah. It is perhaps the most beautiful church in the region. Although small, it is ornate. Even in Bell's day, one can see it was a jewel of Christianity in the region. It is said that the Wise Men from the East, who are mentioned in the Gospels, retired in Hah. Various legends say that there were nine Wise Men. Only three were chosen to follow the star of Bethlehem and find the Christ child. The others remained behind in Hah, waiting for the return of their three brothers. When the three returned they brought a potion of the swaddling clothes of Jesus. They burned the swaddling clothes and the cloth turned into gold medalions with their images emblazoned on each gold piece. There may be some seed of truth in this story as the village is built on top on a more ancient Zoroastrian worship site. Zoroastrians were fire and star worshippers. It very well could be that

Zoroastrians were the ones who are later reported to have visited Jesus in the Holy Land.

Priest and wife of Khah (Hah) with Holy Bible

Close up view of silver cover of church of Hah. This Syriac MS is now located in the private library of the Bishop of Mor Gabriel

Another view of this architectural masterpiece. One can see why Bell was drawn to it.

Bell photographed a group of Kurds who came to meet with her. What is interesting about this picture is that you can see her shadow. She is standing on the wall with the camera help out in front of her.

Bell called this the church of Ibrahim and Urbil near
Midyat

Bishop of Mor Malki (Melko) according to Bell.

Mor Malki

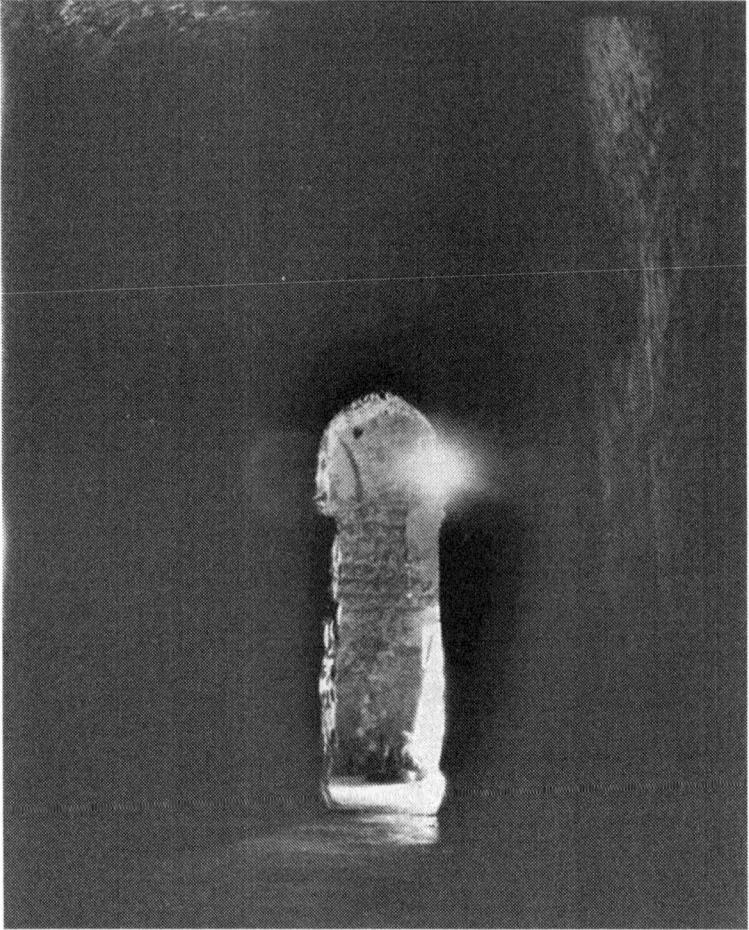

Mor Yuhanna on Mt. Izla

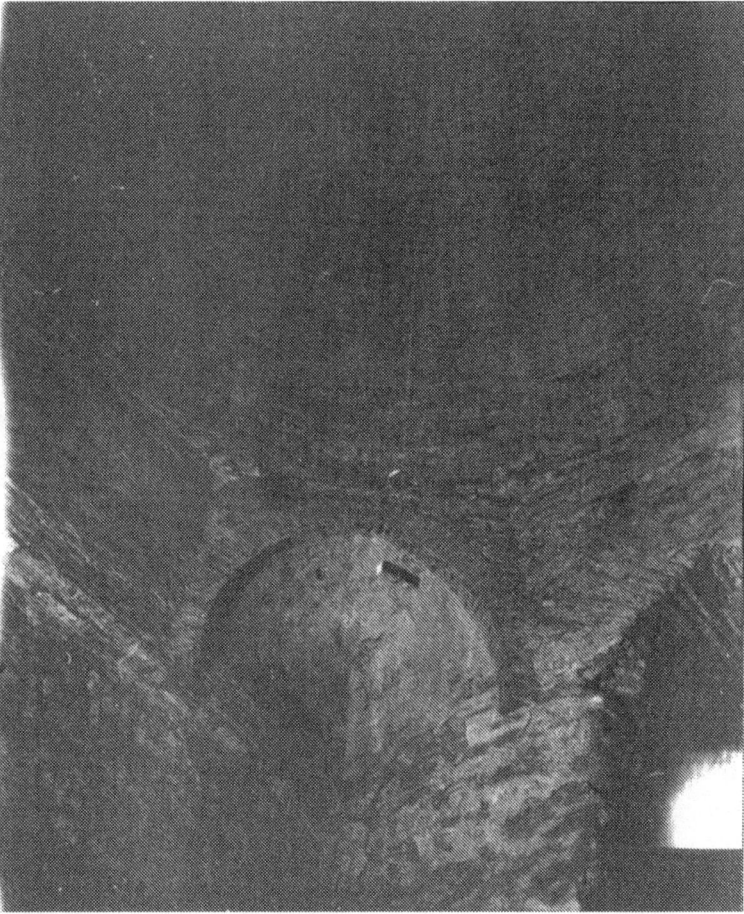

Mor Yuhanna on Mt. Izla.

Monastery on Mt. Izla

On Mt. Izla, once occupied by dozens of monasteries centered around Mor Augen monastery from the 5th century onward.

Salah

Salah

Salah

According to local authorities it this is the grave site of the founders of the monastery of Salah.

Deir Es Salib

Deir Es Salib

Deir es Salib

Exterior view of Deir es Salib

Between Visits

Dear Lord Cromer,

When I was pursuing along the banks of the Euphrates the leisurely course of oriental travel, I would sometimes wonder, sitting at night before my tent door, whether it would be possible to cast into shape the experiences that assailed me. And in that spacious hour, when the silence of the embracing wilderness was enhanced rather than broken by the murmur of the river, and by the sounds, scarcely less primeval, that wavered round the camp fire of my nomad hosts, the task broadened out into a shape which was in keeping with the surroundings. Not only would I set myself to trace the story that was scored upon the face of the earth by mouldering wall or half-choked dyke, by the thousand vestiges of former culture which were scattered about my path, but I would attempt to record the daily life and speech of those who had inherited the empty ground whereon empires had risen and expired. Even there, where the mind ranged out unhindered over the whole wide desert, and thought flowed as smoothly as the flowing stream — even there I would realize the difficulty of such an undertaking, and it was there that I conceived the desire to invoke your aid by setting your name upon the first page of my book. To you, so I promised myself, I could make clear the intention when accomplishment lagged far behind it. To you the very landscape would be familiar, though you had never set eyes upon it: the river and the waste which determined, as in your country of the Nile, the direction of mortal energies. And you, with your profound experience of the East, have learnt to reckon with the unbroken continuity of its history. Conqueror follows upon the heels of conqueror, nations are overthrown and cities topple down into the dust, but the conditions of exist- / *p. viii* / ence are unaltered and irresistibly they fashion the new age in the likeness of the old. "Amurath an Amurath succeeds" and the tale is told again.

161

Where past and present are woven so closely together, the habitual appreciation of the divisions of time slips insensibly away. Yesterday's raid and an expedition of Shalmaneser fall into the same plane; and indeed what essential difference lies between them? But the reverberation of ancient fame sounds more richly in the ears than the voice of modern achievement. The banks of the Euphrates echo with ghostly alarums; the Mesopotamian deserts are full of the rumour of phantom armies; you will not blame me if I passed among them "trattando l'ombre come cosa salda."

And yet there was a new note. For the first time in all the turbulent centuries to which those desolate regions bear witness, a potent word had gone forth, and those who had caught it listened in amazement, asking one another for an explanation of its meaning. Liberty — what is liberty? I think the question that ran so perplexingly through the black tents would have received no better a solution in the royal pavilions which had once spread their glories over the plain. Idly though it fell from the lips of the Bedouin, it foretold change. That sense of change, uneasy and bewildered, hung over the whole of the Ottoman Empire. It was rarely unalloyed with anxiety; there was, it must be admitted, little to encourage an unqualified confidence in the immediate future. But one thing was certain: the moving Finger had inscribed a fresh title upon the page. I cannot pretend to a judicial indifference in this matter. I have drawn too heavily upon the good-will of the inhabitants of Asiatic Turkey to regard their fortunes with an impartial detachment. I am eager to seize upon promise and slow to be overmastered by disappointment. But I should be doing an equivocal service to a people who have given me so full a measure of hospitality and fellowship if I were to underestimate the problems that lie before them. The victories of peace are more laborious than those of war. They demand a higher integrity than that which has been practised hitherto in Turkey, and a finer conception of citizenship than any which has been current there. The old tyranny has lifted, but it has left its shadow over the land.

The five months of journeying which are recounted in this book were months of suspense and even of terror. Constitutional government trembled in the balance and was like to be outweighted by the forces of disorder, by fanaticism, massacre and civil strife. I saw the latest Amurath succeed to Amurath and rejoiced with all those who love justice and freedom to hear him proclaimed. For 'Abdu'l Hamîd, helpless as he may then have been in the hands of the weavers of intrigue, was the symbol for retrogression, and the triumph of his faction must have extinguished the faint light that had dawned upon his empire.

The confused beginnings which I witnessed were the translation of a generous ideal into the terms of human imperfection. Nowhere was the character of the Young Turkish movement recognized more fully than in England, and nowhere did it receive a more disinterested sympathy. Our approval was not confined to words. We have never been slow to welcome and to encourage the advancement of Turkey, and I am glad to remember that we were the first to hold out a helping hand when we saw her struggling to throw off long-established evils. If she can win a place, with a strong and orderly government, among civilized states, turning her face from martial adventure and striving after the reward that waits upon good administration and sober industry, the peace of the world will be set upon a surer basis, and therein lies our greatest advantage as well as her own. That day may yet be far off, but when it comes, as I hope it will, perhaps some one will take down this book from the shelf and look back, not without satisfaction, upon the months of revolution which it chronicles. And remembering that the return of prosperity to the peoples of the near East began with your administration in Egypt, he will understand why I should have ventured to offer it, with respectful admiration, to you.

GERTRUDE LOWTHIAN BELL.

1910

January 9th, 1911.

Two things I want in Rome.

You know the round church of Santa Costanza) outside the walls? Next to it is the little basilica of St. Agnese which has in the inside a double storey of columns on either side of the nave. The capitals of the lower story are acanthus captals with tiny garlands hung over the corners. I want a photograph of one of these, showing the garland clearly, for it is the only example I know in Rome of the garlanded capital of the early Christian monuments at Diarbekr and in the Tur Abdin. The photograph does not, I think, exist. But Eugénie's photographer would take it for me for a few francs. I shall want it as a point for comparison when I write my forthcoming work about the Tur Abdin.

1911: **Return to Tur Abdin**

Bell returned to the Tur Abdin region in April of 1911.

[14 April 1911]

[14 April 1911] Ap. 14. Dearest Mother. I posted a long letter to you on April 3, the day I arived at K. Shergat [Sharqat], since when I regret to observe that I have not written at all. I spent three enchanting days at K. Shergat and would gladly have stayed longer - they, also, wd gladly have kept me - but I had on my conscience much work to be done in the Tur 'Abdin. Three of the 4 who were there 2 years ago I found this year, and two others whom I had not seen before. One of them, Herr Preusser, had visited two of my Tur 'Abdin churches and is publishing them, so we had a great time comparing plans and discussing the various theories we had formed. But chiefly I found this year, as I found 2 years ago, great profit from endless talks with Dr Andrae. His knowledge of Mesopotamian problems is so great and his views so brilliant and comprehensive. We went over the whole ground again with such additional matter as I had brought from Kasr i Shirin [Qasr-e-Shirin] (it is all a part of the same story) and as he had derived from two more years of digging at Assur [Ashur] and from his work at Hatra [Hadr, Al]. He put everything at my disposal, photographs and unpublished plans and his own unpublished ideas. I don't think that many people are so generous. Also they taught me to photograph by flash light and provided me with the material for doing so, which I shall find very useful in some of my pitch dark churches. And we went over the last two years' work stone by stone and discussed it in all its bearings. K. Shergat was looking its best, all clothed in grass and flowers. I love it better than any ruined site in the world, but perhaps that is mainly because of the gratitude and affection which I feel towards my hosts there. The only drawback of my visit was that I was so reluctant to go away, and I carried a heavy heart over the high desert to Hatra - which is a long way. But one can't be heavy hearted at Hatra; it is too wonderfully interesting. It was (perhaps you know?) the capital city of the Parthian kings, about whom we know so little. Septimus Severus besieged it and it was finally overthrown by the Sasanian Sapor, in the year AD 360, if I remember right. Sapor's ditch and mound are still to be seen enclosing the ruins of the city wall. It was never reinhabited and it lies out on the stretching downs like the great ground plan of a city, grass grown walls and mounds marking the line of fortification, street and market. In the centre stands the palace - you can see it for 5 hours away on every side - immense stone built halls, roofed with huge vaults and decorated with the strangest carved ornaments that have ever grown out under oriental chisels. The Parthians were an eclectic folk; their arts sprang up on ground that had already been strongly Hellenized by the Alexandrids, and they learnt, no doubt, from the Romans, with whom they were always at war. They worked out these new ideas upon old oriental foundations and the palace at Hatra is the one building left out of all their cities, where you can see the results at which they arrived, for it stands to this day. We arrived late on a grey and stormy afternoon and were received with acclamation by the Turkish army. The modern conditions at Hatra were this year almost as exciting as the ancient. It had been the centre of comprehensive and entirely successful operations for the pacification of the desert and about

300 of the 1500 men who had been sent up from Baghdad in January were still there when I arrived. The object of the expedition had been to bring the Shammar to order, and the Shammar are the most important of the N. Mesopotamian tribes. Riza Beg, who was in command, took the sheikhs by surprise. Without firing a shot he forced about 15000 of the tribe to come in to Hatra, levied, in kind, the long unpaid taxes, settled all grievances and appointed a single sheikh over the whole tribe who is to be responsible for the good behaviour of all. He himself returned to Baghdad - summoned in haste by Nazim Pasha, but too late to prevent his fall - and the greater part of the troops have gone further west to treat with those sheikhs who could not come to Hatra on account of inter tribal blood feud. The whole business has been brilliantly well done and I think that if the government has a few more men like Riza Beg (which it has) and knows how to use them, the whole desert will shortly be as safe as any city. I shall write a long article for some leading journal when I get home and call it The Pacification of the Desert, for it should be known how well and wisely the Turks are handling matters here. The men whom I saw at Hatra had been 3 months in camp under exceptionally difficult conditions, for no sooner had Riza Beg arrived than the snow fell and all communications were blocked for 3 weeks. The Pasha did not turn a hair. He kept his men alive for 3 weeks on sheep and dates, he kept them in good spirits by his own intrepid example and he carried his job through as though it were a picnic party. I wish I had seen him; he must be a very remarkable man. The troops when I came were in excellent trim, saddlery all clean, arms all bright; they had lost only one man from sickness, but they had had, not unnaturally, a pretty heavy loss in horses.

The only criticism one can make is that the whole camp was absolutely innocent of sanitary arrangements; the ruins were unspeakably dirty and even the dead horses lay half buried (if buried at all) in close proximity to the tents. Hatra had been turned into a base camp for the further operations on the Khabur, where the rest of the troops had gone, and the officers and men were having rather a dull time; they were therefore very glad to see me and to hear the news from Baghdad. I had plenty to give them. There were Turks and Arabs and Kurds among them, at every stage of civilization, so to speak: some fresh from a German schooling in Constantinople [Istanbul] and some who had never had any schooling at all. They were all delightful. I made special friends with a young lieutenant of a mountain battery who had joined two years ago and had spent the whole time of his service on important military expeditions against the Arabs. A more charming boy, you can't imagine. The immediate future of the Turkish empire depends, to my mind, entirely on what the soldiers are like, for it is carefully to be remembered that the whole work of government is at this moment military, and will be for some time to come, that is till the country is internally at peace. And for education and integrity the officers are head and shoulders above every other body of men in Turkey. But perhaps I might as well reserve the rest of my observations for the article. So I spent a day at Hatra, mainly in photographing, a terrible business because there was so much of it. The Parthians had carved round every arched doorway of their halls heads of men and animals, and sometimes little figures, dimly reminiscent of classical reliefs: there was one Eros that might almost have come from a Greek hand. These strings of heads over Roman mouldings and barbaric acanthus leaves give me the most bewildering impression of a jumble of the arts. And more curious still, high up on the walls in the interior of the halls they set huge heads in groups of three, and these too are sometimes dimly classical, a Medusa head, a bearded river god; and sometimes they are wild and staring masks, scarcely human. But the abiding impression of the place is its immense size, the splendid solidity of its stone work and the daring sweep of its vaults. We pitched our camp close to Riza Beg's empty tent, outside the military lines, and I was nearly shot down by a sentinel when I strolled in innocently the first night to drink a cup of coffee with the Commandant. After I had done my work we paraded the army, cavalry, infantry and artillery, and I photographed them all, to their great satisfaction - and to mine. The drawback of Hatra is the water. It's all salt. The town stands about half an hour from the river Tharthar [Tharthar, Wadi ath] which is so bitter salt that no one drinks it but the Arabs; we drank from wells, but they were exceedingly nasty. When I left I was escorted for a couple of hours by half a dozen officers who galoped [sic] with me across the beautiful grass plains; we drew up on a mound and waited for the caravan, and then we took a tender farewell of one another and I went on more soberly with my own men. We followed the Tharthar valley and fortunately in an hour or two came to a rain water pool (there had been a good deal of rain the day before) at which we filled a skin. It was even more horrid, I thought, than the Hatra salt water, sticky greasy standing water, tasting strongly of decayed grass. But we had nothing else. There were Arab camps and flocks all along the shallow valley and we camped at evening near some of these. There was abundant grass, but we had no fresh water for the horses, and all but my mare refused to drink the

Tharthar water. I could not wonder, for it tasted like the sea. It was a very delicious camping ground but I was rather disturbed because Fattuh was ill. He has from time to time terribly violent neuralgia - I suppose it is - and it breaks my heart to see him in such dreadful pain. We had a difficult journey next day. Fattuh was very ill and we had a march of nearly 11 hours which we could not shorten because there was no fresh water. We passed a rain pool in the morning, watered our horses and took a skinful with us, but the day was hot and the men thirsty and by 5 o'clock there was scarcely any left. The Jebel Sinjar [Sinjar, Jabal], to which we were going, was still an immense way off and I began to wonder whether Fattuh would get through the day. He never complained, bless him, but every now and then he stopped and lay down for a minute or two and then caught us up silently. At last we saw Arab tents ahead and knew that there must be drinkable water near at hand. We put up our tents near them, boiled water and made hot compresses for Fattuh and forced him to lie down while the muleteers made shift to cook some sort of dinner. The Arabs were very sympathetic and brought us some curds and milk, but the water they had was next to undrinkable, drawn from standing rain pools. Next morning Fattuh was a little better. I sent him with the caravan straight to Balad Sinjar [Sinjar] - it was only about 6 hours away - and taking one of the muleteers with me and an Arab guide rode off to a more eastern point where there stands a very interesting ruined Khan which I wanted to photograph. I was well rewarded for besides the carved gateway which I knew of there was a most exciting parallel to the Ukheidir [Ukhaydir] vaulting system which I have never found before in any later building. And I don't suppose it has struck other people, because, not knowing Ukheidir, they can't have been on the watch for it. Moreover we joined company with a body of the Shammar who were on their way northwards from Riza Beg's gathering of the clan at Hatra. They were moving camp when I came up to them and the whole world was alive with their camels. Now the Shammar are Bedu; only the Shammar and the 'Anazeh are real Bedawin, the others are just Arabs. Ahl el ba'Œr we call the Bedu, the People of the Camel. They never cultivate the soil or stay more than a night or two in one place, but wander ceaselessly over the inner desert. It was delightful to see their women and children travelling in the camel howdahs and their men carrying the long spears that are planted before the tent door. They talk a speech of their own: we had a long conversation at the Khan where some of them stopped to watch me photograph. When that was done I sent back my guide and 'Abud and I jogged peacefully along under the hills till we came to Balad Sinjar, early in the afternoon, and found our camp pitched under the town near to a swift clear mountain stream. Fattuh had called in the services of a native's doctor who had copiously bled him, not a cure I should have recommended, but it (or time) seems to have been effective, for the neuralgia has gone. The Sinjar mountains are inhabited mainly by Yezidis, which, you remember, are devil worshippers. Until a couple of years ago the Yezidis were ceaselessly at war with the Arabs, and with everybody else, but the Turks have now put in what seems to be a really effectual government, raiding has almost stopped and the roads are quite safe. It is the same story everywhere you see. I should have had nothing to fear in any case for being a friend (and lately a guest) of 'Ali Beg, the head of all Yezidis, I should have been certain of a good reception. However it was not necessary to press my claims upon their hospitality; the government officials were more than sufficient. I paid, however, a visit on the head Yezidi sheikh, but as he could talk nothing but Kurdish, we had to converse through the medium of an official who had come with me. The officer in command was a very pleasant young Turk who had come out with Nazim Pasha and much regretted his fall. There was also a charming kaimmakam, a Damascene, who was deeply interested in the antiquities of the mountain, had read all the Arab inscriptions on the old buildings and gave me a lot of information. The town itself, though it is now a mean village hanging on the slopes of a little foothill, was in the Middle Ages a very considerable place, and its ruins stretch far down into the plain, minarets and tombs of fine Arab work. It was a frontier fort of the Roman Empire when Septimus Severus carried his rule into Mesopotamia, and it was held by the Persians before it fell to the Arabs. It was raining heavily the next morning and I wanted to see more of Balad Sinjar, so I was glad of the excuse for staying a day there. I spent most of the morning with the kaimmakam and after lunch rode up a wild rocky gorge to a place called Deir el 'Asi, the {Rebellious} Unruly Cloister - so called, I suppose, because of its situation for the road to it is almost impassable. The monastery, if monastery it was, consists of a number of caves, finely hollowed out of the rock, great chambers leading the one into the other, and sometimes two storeys of them. A little spring breaks out of the rock below and a few trees grow by it. There is no road beyond, though you can climb up into the mountain top over the crags. The caves are inhabited by Yezidis who scrape together some sort of subsistence among the rocks - Heaven knows how they contrive to live. We got back to our tents just as a very heavy shower of rain fell, and congratulated ourselves on having escaped the worst of it. I had tea and was sitting waiting for the Kaimmakam, who was coming to call, when suddenly a hail storm battered onto my tent roof. I began hastily to fasten the door and before you could wink a hurricane of wind swept down upon us and every tent was flat. My books and papers went flying out into the universe, Fattuh and Abud flying after them, while I, half blinded with wind and hail, strapped up our open boxes. It only lasted for a minute or two, but we were all wet through. We gathered ourselves together and began putting up the tents again - the casualties were extraordinarily small: a tent pole, an eyeglass and a comb, and a good many odds and ends of papers, nothing very important. The 2 muleteers came running down from the town, where they had (fortunately for themselves) been buying corn, the tents were got up again, the sun came out and we changed and spread out our wet things to dry. It was an extremely disagreeable experience, but what we should have done if it had happened at night I can't think. You may imagine how we lay awake and listened to every gust of wind! There were plenty, but none so bad as the tornado of the afternoon. I had wanted to cut straight across the mountains and make a bee line to Nisibin [Nusaybin (Nisibis)], but I was told that I could not take a caravan over and from what I had seen of the roads I thought it probable that this was true. So we rode westwards under the southern slope of the mountain and late in the afternoon turned north over a low pass and camped just over the brow of it by a stream. There was a Yezidi tent village above us and great fine crags on either side. Also it was mountain cold. It had rained on and off all day and it rained and blew all night, but our tents were firmly anchored. I have two delightful zaptiehs with me from Balad Sinjar - gendarmes we call them in these modern days. One of them explained to me as we rode the whole duty of the Jon Darma, upon whom, as he rightly said, the working of the Ottoman Empire mainly rests. "And that is why we are called Jon Darma" said Muhammad Chowwish. "It is because they say to us 'Darma!' Darma in Turkish means don't stop. I did not ask what he thought Jon meant. Today it was mostly fine but very cold. We came down out of our mountain and rode straight north over wonderful grass plains with black tents scattered over them, and herds of grazing camels - the tents of the Tayy Arabs with a few Shammar skulking among them in the hope that they may escape the soldiers on the Khabur; we know them by their speech. We have camped under a big mound, or rather on the slopes of it to avoid the marsh which occupies all the low ground here. We have the Sinjar mountains to the south and the Tur Abdin, which ends Mesopotamia, to the north, but I doubt we shall have weary riding through the marsh tomorrow. Meantime we have completed our drying; my shoes and books were still sopping wet from the Sinjar storm. The camp fires of the Tayy gleam round the horizon like glow worms: at its best moments the desert is a difficult place to beat for beauty. But it was not at its best this morning. We rode for 3 hours almost continuously through heaps of dead sheep and donkeys. They had died in the snow, whole flocks of the them together, and there they lay. I saw one or two dead gazelles and in places the ground was strewn with dead birds. The cold, however, had done no harm to the scorpions which abound in this district. We killed 5 round about our tents - too many.

Saturday Ap 15. [15 April 1911]

Saturday Ap 15. [15 April 1911] After all we had no trouble from the mud, but arrived at Nisibin [Nusaybin (Nisibis)] after a pleasant and easy march of 8 hours, all across grass plains. Nisibin is now a tiny village lying in the midst of the ruin heaps which were once the greatest fortified city of the Roman frontier. There is a vivid account in Ammianus Marcellinus of the despair of the inhabitants when they heard that Jovian had handed over their city to Sapor in the disgraceful peace he made with the Persians after Julian's death. I wish I had the book with me; I should like to read it again here. A. Marcellinus is a great scene painter; the story lives again as you read him. We have camped by some big columns that stand knee deep in the ground, crowned with battered Corinthian capitals. No one knows to what building they belonged. The only other thing that remains here is a fragment of a wonderfully interesting church at which I propose to work tomorrow morning. It is sister to my Tur Abdin churches but I think a younger sister. The Tur Abdin mountains are about 4 miles to the north of us - wonderfully beautiful now in a soft evening light. A pair of storks are nesting on top of my columns. They are a little doubtful as to whether they like us.

Monday Ap 17. [17 April 1911]

Monday Ap 17. [17 April 1911] There is a charming passage in Sir Edward Grey's book on fly fishing in which he praises the various moods of Nature. "Rain" says he "is delightful" and I remember when I read it, thinking of warm May rain on our opening beech leaves at home and thoroughly agreeing with him. But one begins to feel rather differently about it when one is camping in pitiless torrents. It rained like the devil on Saturday night and like ten thousand devils on Sunday. The wind howled through my tent ropes till it sounded like a hurricane on board ship, and the rain thundered against the canvass [sic]. I thought my tent would go down more than once, but my excellent servants kept the pegs firm by piling stones onto them. The storks were less fortunate: their house was blown away. The wind went down a little at midday and I spent the afternoon working at the church which is windowless anyway and therefore no darker in cloudy weather than in fine. The rain stopped after a bit and the evening was fine, but you have a comfortless damp sort of feeling in tents that have been so thoroughly drenched. It rained on and off all today but fortunately the 5 hours during which we were on the road to Dara was an off time. About an hour or so out of Nisibin [Nusaybin (Nisibis)] I caught sight of 5 European tents pitched near a village a mile from the road. I galoped [sic] down to see who those travellers were and was made welcome by 5 engineers, 2 Frenchmen and 3 Germans who are making the final survey for this bit of the Baghdad rly. It is to reach Nisibin in 3 years. I spent an hour talking to them and longed to ask what agreement, if any, has been reached with us on the subject of the Baghdad section, but I did not like to open that thorny issue and probably they knew no more than I. What a change the coming of the rly will make here! I cannot help regretting, in a way, the passing of the old order, but it is passed and it is high time that the rly came to strengthen the new. So we rode on by tracks deep in mud to Dara, which was one of the strongest of Justinian's frontier fortresses. I found my camp pitched just inside the ruined wall and though it was raining a little I took a guide and wandered about for a couple of hours among the ruins. There is not very much above ground, but underground you can still see the huge vaulted cisterns which were planned and built by a Greek architect from Alexandria whom Justinian employed on this job. There is a small Christian community and I called upon the Armenian priest and then hurried home because the rain was beginning to fall again so heavily. It's going to be a pig of a night.

[25 April 1911]

[25 April 1911] Ap 25 Tuesday Dearest Mother. I posted a letter to you the day I arrived in Mardin and told you that the kind American missionaries had taken me in. I spent 2 days with them and enjoyed my visit very much. One of my hosts, an old party called Andrus, is the man who knows the Tur Abdin better than any other person and to him is due most of the mapping of the country. I had profitable talks with him. The first day of my stay I rode out early to a famous monastery called Deir Zafran, about an hour and a half from Mardin. It was a wonderful ride along the face of the hills with the great plain below us. That plain seen from Mardin and the high mountain roads about the town is the most glorious thing I ever beheld, more beautiful than the sea, and, when I saw it, perpetually varied by the storms that came sweeping over it. The monastery was very interesting, 8th century I should think and full of exciting decoration. I photographed diligently, having received permission to do what I liked by an aged bishop, and when I had finished my work and spent the rest of the afternoon sightseeing in Mardin. Next day I went up to the castle which crowns the rock 500 ft above the town - an inconceivably splendid fortress. A missionary boy came with me and in the afternoon we visited a beautiful Moslem medresseh outside the town. Everything is beautiful in Mardin because everything faces the immense plain. But the dirt of the town is past words. The houses are all cut back into the rock, the roof of one on a level with the threshold of the next. The streets are narrow staircases piled with dirt. This winter Mardin was cut off from the rest of the world for 47 days - it was as bad as a siege. The snow, shovelled off the house roofs, filled the narrow streets and was piled up in places above the houses - there was no other place to put it. No one in Europe can realize what a helpless Oriental population suffers under exceptional conditions such as these. Everyone to whom I talked told me how much the American missionaries had done, and indeed it was they who opened the road, the government being paralyzed into complete inaction. I left Mardin on the 21st, and rode eastward into the Tur Abdin. It is no wonder that the armies of Persian [sic] and Byzantine left it in peace; the mountain is to this day almost impassible. We scrambled all day up and down steep and rocky hills. There is no method in them; the deep waterless valleys run in all directions and until you get to Midyat there is no open ground. We camped at a tiny Kurdish village and no sooner had we got our tents up than torrents of rain fell upon us. It was very damp and cold; but that was the end of the bad weather and it has been exquisite ever since. I had an interesting day's ride into Midyat. I had heard at my camping place of ruins and in order to see them went through a district which has I think been visited by no European. The paths were execrable but I was rewarded by finding a pre-Christian building, 3rd century AD I should think (Pagan I mean) with some wonderful decoration on it and secondly two very ancient shrines, partly rock cut and partly build of huge blocks of stone. I can't date these as they are unlike anything I have seen, but they were immensely interesting and I planned and photographed them with great satisfaction. Nearly every village in the Tur Abdin has a sacred grove by it, a stretch of ground where the oak scrub is allowed to grow into respectable trees. They bury their dead in or about it and it is hallowed by a pile of stones which is supposed to represent the grave of a pious person of old times - I wonder into what dim mists of antiquity the sanctity of these sites really extends! We got into Midyat after sunset, having worked and travelled for 13 hours (too long I think) and found the camp pitched and dinner ready. I rode out early next day and worked at two of the churches I had planned before. Thank Heaven I have been over that work again for it was too hastily done and I found many mistakes. Yesterday, on my way to Deir el 'Amr, I called on the Chelabi and thanked him for his kind intervention in the robbery 2 years ago. They never caught the robbers, by the way! But the Govt. seized all the sheep of the village to which they belonged and sold them - for which I am not sorry. We camped at Deir el 'Amr, high up on the tops of the hills and I worked like a nigger all the afternoon. But my plan was not so bad here. It is a fine place. And so today we came on to Kefrzeh and camped again on a hill top under as splendid a 5th century church as you would wish to see. I went over my plan again - it was pretty accurate - and took a lot more photographs. The population is mostly Christian here, charming people who all welcomed me like an old friend. There is an old nun here whom I saw 2 years ago. I accordingly revived our acquaintance with a small tip; whereupon she sent me a gift of eggs and bread and we responded suitably with an offering of sugar. The Sheikh of the village was very kind and attentive and insisted on spending the night near our tents to watch over us.

Photos of 1911 Visit

Nisibis bridge

Nisibis: Mor Jacob Church

Nisibis: Mor Jacob Church

Nisibis

Nisibis: Interior Mor Jacob

Nisibis: Mor Jacob

Nisisbis: Mor Jacob

Post Spring Equinox light cast through a shaft window of Zoroastrian origin. This is one of the evidences.

Mardin

Evidence of 5th century construction at Deir Zaferon

Southwestern wall of sanctuary

Deir Zaferon sanctuary

Northeastern corner of sanctuary

Eastern wall of Deir Zaferon sanctuary

Maps

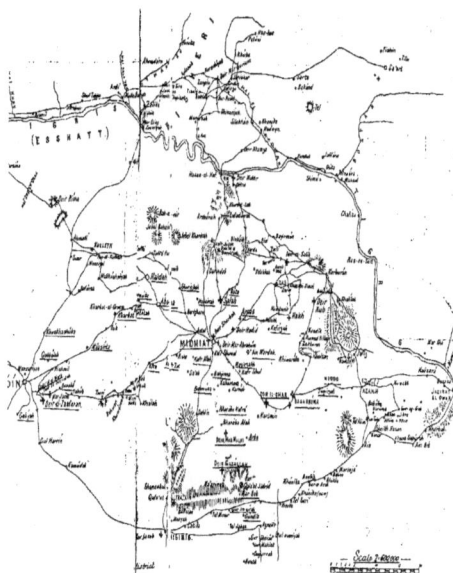

Expedition Map of the general areas of Bell first and second visit to Tur Abdin

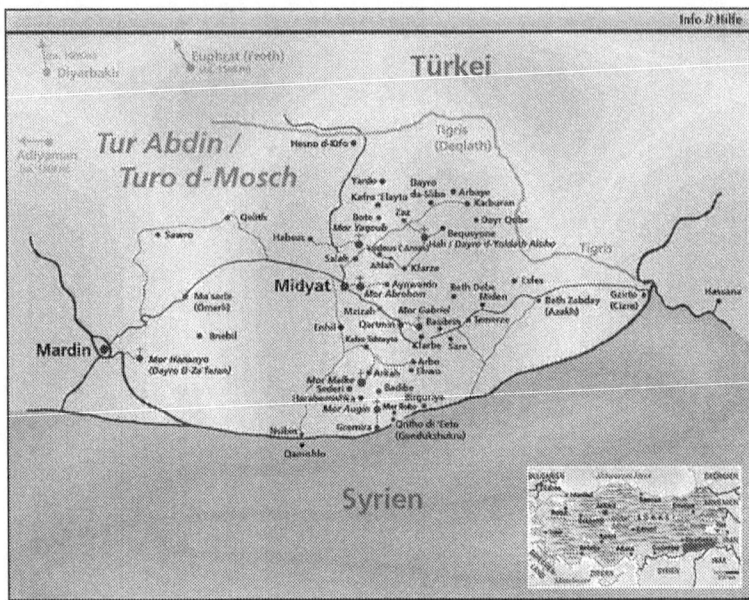

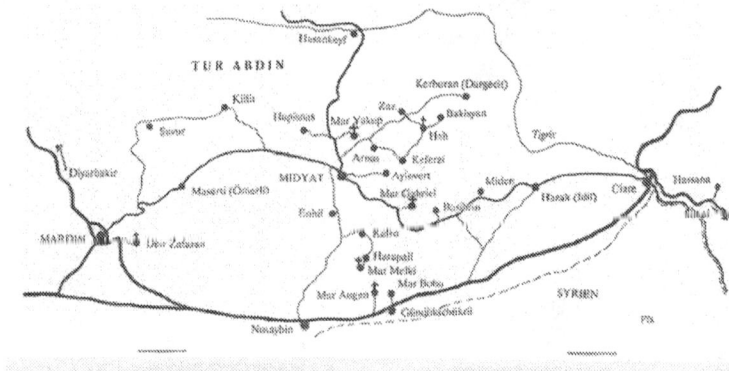

Maps of Tur Abdin

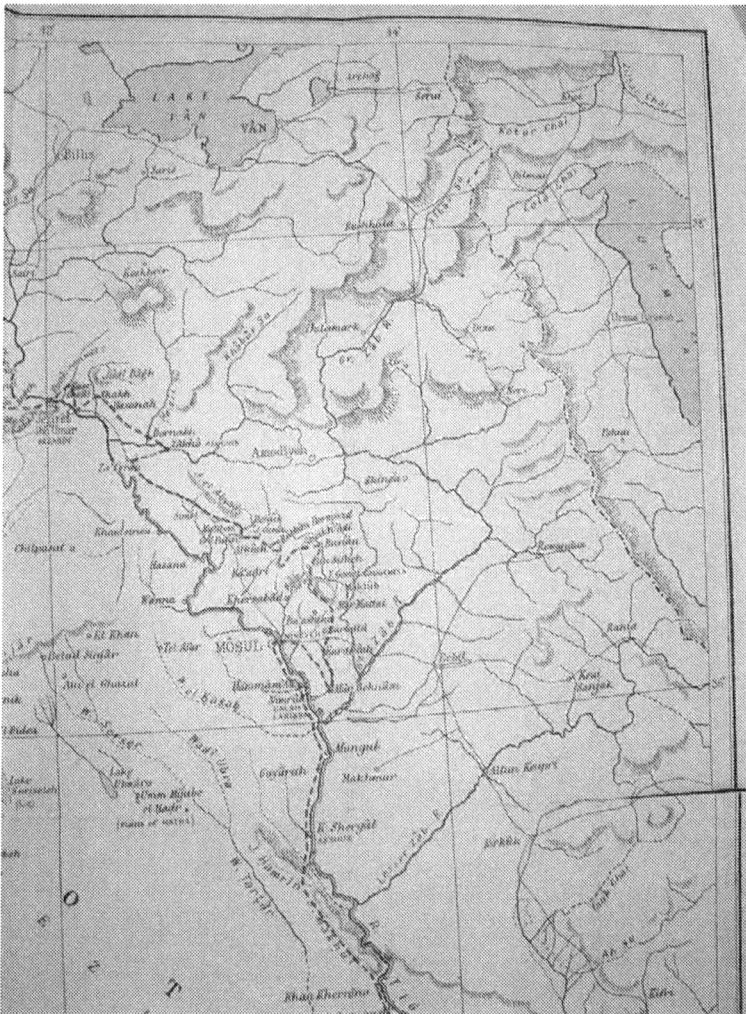

Upper left area is where Bell enters Tur Abdin on first visit.

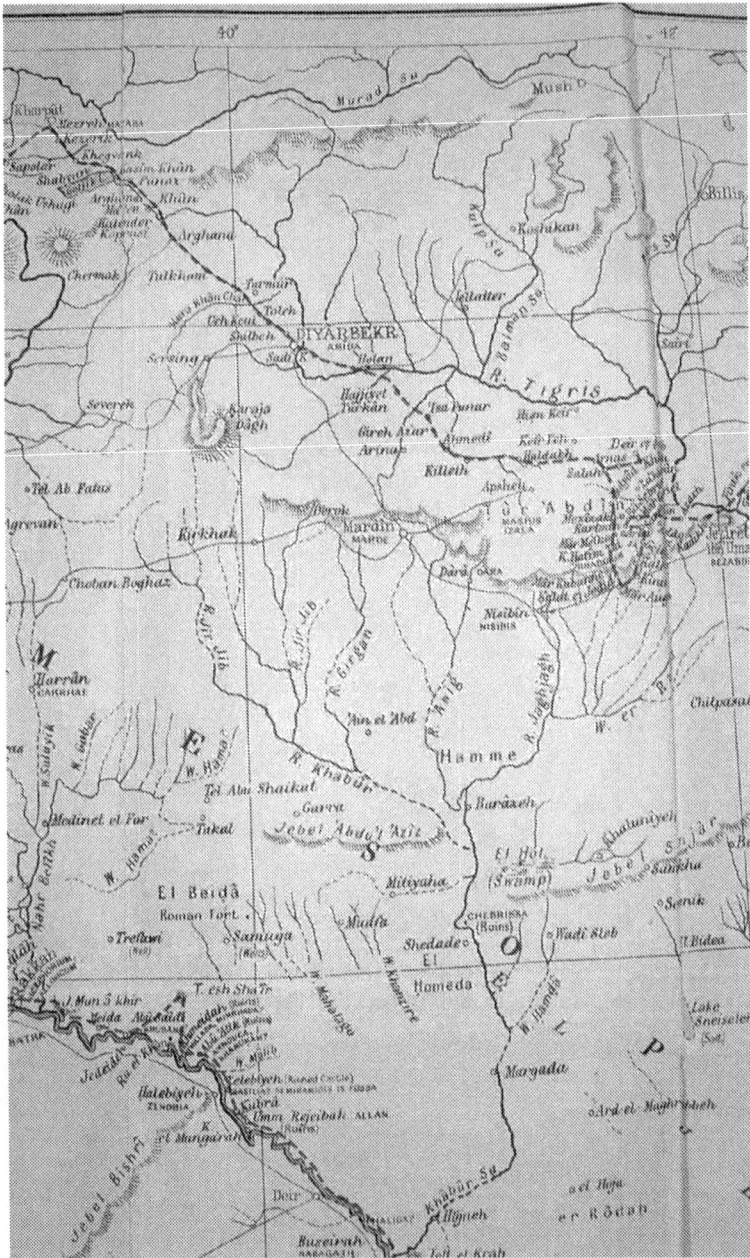

196

Upper line from right to left follows the remainder of first visit ending in Diyarbakir.

www.ingramcontent.com/pod-product-compliance
Lightning Source LLC
Chambersburg PA
CBHW031256090426
42742CB00007B/474